WITHDRAWN

THE BLUE CLIFF RECORD

VOLUME THREE

The Blue Cliff Record

Translated from the Chinese *Pi Yen Lu* by
Thomas and J. C. Cleary

SHAMBHALA
Boulder & London
1977

SHAMBHALA PUBLICATIONS, INC.
1123 Spruce Street
Boulder, Colorado 80302

© 1977 by Thomas & J. C. Cleary.
All rights reserved.
ISBN 0-87773-112-8
LCC 76-14202

Distributed in the United States by Random House
and in Canada by Random House of Canada Ltd.

Distributed in the Commonwealth by Routledge &
Kegan Paul Ltd., London and Henley-on-Thames

Printed in the United States of America

Contents

The Blue Cliff Record III

774249

Biographical Supplement

Original Preface to The Blue Cliff Record

The lifeline of the perfect sages, the great capacity of the successive Patriarchs, the miraculous method of changing the bones, the wondrous art of nourishing the spirit—the Ch'an Master Hsueh Tou had the true eye which transcends any sect and goes beyond patterns; he upheld the true imperative and did not reveal a customary standard. He took up the hammer and tongs to smelt and forge Buddhas and Patriarchs, and versified the transcendental noses of the patchrobed monks. A silver mountain, an iron wall; who could dare try to bore in? A mosquito trying to bite an iron ox cannot manage to penetrate. If you do not meet a great Master, how can you thoroughly comprehend the abstruse subtleties?

Here there is an old man, Yuan Wu; when he was dwelling at the Blue Cliff, students were confused and asked him for instruction. The old man pitied them and therefore extended his compassion; he dug out the profound source and elucidated the underlying principles. Directly pointing at the ultimate, how could he have set up any opinionated understanding? The hundred public cases are pierced through on one thread from the beginning; the whole crowd of old fellows are all judged in turn.

You should know that the jewel of Chao was flawless to begin with; Hsiang Ju brazenly fooled the king of Ch'in. The ultimate path is in reality wordless; masters of our school extend compassion to rescue the fallen. If you see it like this, only then do you realize their thoroughgoing kindness. If, on the other hand, you get stuck on the phrases and sunk in the words, you won't avoid exterminating the Buddha's race.

P'u Chao was fortunate to be close to the Master's seat and was able to hear what he had never heard before. Companions in the Way compiled it into a volume, and this stupid oaf has reported the root and branches of the matter.

At the time it is the last day of the month in late spring,

1128. The monk P'u Chao, a participant in the study and successor to the Patriarchs, humbly writes this preface.

*　*　*　*　*　*　*

A long time ago a king offered to trade fifteen cities to another king in exchange for a single jewel. When the emissary came with the jewel and handed it over, he saw that the first king was reluctant to part with his cities; he then recovered the jewel by claiming it was flawed and threatened to smash it unless the king honored his part of the bargain, whereat the king relented. Unless we are willing to give up our attachments, we cannot appreciate the priceless jewel of our true nature. Each case of the Blue Cliff Record shows us not only where to find the jewel, but also how to dig it out and cut and polish it to bring out its inherent beauty and magnificence.

Kuei Shan Attends on Pai Chang

POINTER

For a fast man, a single word; for a fast horse, a single stroke of the whip. Ten thousand years, one thought; one thought, ten thousand years. You must know directly before it is raised.

But say, before it is raised, how will you search for it? I'm citing this old case: look!

CASE

Kuei Shan, Wu Feng, and Yun Yen were together attending on Pai Chang.[1] Pai Chang asked Kuei Shan, "With your throat, mouth, and lips shut, how will you speak?"[2]

Kuei Shan said, "Please, Teacher, you speak instead."[3]

Chang said, "I don't refuse to speak to you, but I fear that (if I did) in the future I would be bereft of descendants."[4]

NOTES

1. Haha! From beginning to end obscure and hard to understand. You're headed west, I'm going east.
2. One general is hard to find.
3. Kuei Shan proceeds by Pai Chang's road.
4. He doesn't avoid grandmotherly kindness. The skin on his face is three inches thick. He mingles and mixes with mud and water. He goes right up and takes him.

COMMENTARY

Kuei Shan, Wu Feng, and Yun Yen were together attending on Pai Chang. Pai Chang asked Kuei Shan, "With your throat, mouth, and lips shut, how will you speak?" Shan said, "Please, Teacher, you speak instead." Chang said, "I don't refuse to

473

speak to you, but I fear that (if I did) in the future I would be bereft of descendants." Although Pai Chang acted like this, his pot had already been carried off by someone else. He also asked Wu Feng (this same question). Feng said, "Teacher, you too should shut up." Chang said, "Where there's no one, I shade my eyes with my hand and gaze out towards you." He also asked Yun Yen. Yen said, "Teacher, do you have (any way to speak) or not?" Chang said, "I have lost my descendants." Each of these three men was a Master.

An Ancient said, "On the level ground there are dead people without number. Those who can pass through the forest of brambles are the skillful ones." Therefore teachers of our school use the forest of brambles to test people. Why? They couldn't test people if they stuck to phrases based on ordinary feelings. Patchrobed monks must be able to display their ability in phrases and discern the point within words. As for board-carrying fellows, they often die within the words and say, "If throat, mouth, and lips are shut, there's no longer a way to say anything." As for those who can adapt successfully, they have waves which go against the current, they have a single road right in the question. They don't cut their hands blundering against its sharp point.

Kuei Shan said, "Please, Teacher, you speak instead." Tell me, what did he mean? Here he was like sparks struck from stone, like a flash of lightning: pressing back against Pai Chang's question, he answered immediately. He had his own way to get himself out, without wasting the slightest effort. Thus it is said, "He studies the living phrase; he doesn't study the dead phrase."

Nevertheless, Pai Chang did not take him up on it, but just said, "I don't refuse to speak to you, but I fear that (if I did) in the future I would be bereft of descendants." Whenever teachers of our school help people, they pull out nails and extract pegs. As for people these days who say that this answer doesn't approve of Kuei Shan and doesn't comprehend his words, how far they are from knowing that right here is the one path of his living potential, towering up like a thousand-fathom wall, interchanging guest and host, leaping with life.

Hsueh Tou likes these words of Kuei Shan's, likes his freedom to revolve around and maneuver elegantly while still being able to hold fast to his territory. Therefore his verse says:

VERSE

"Please, Teacher, you speak instead."
> This contains the universe. He's already cut his hand
> against the sharp point.

The tiger's head sprouts horns as he emerges from the wild
*   weeds.*
> Very startling indeed. Undeniably, he's extraordinary.

On the ten continents spring ends and the flowers fade and
*   wither—*
> Everywhere is pure and cool. No praise is sufficient.

Over the coral forest the sun is dazzling bright.
> (In the coral branches the light is reflected) a hundred-
> fold, a thousand-fold. Nevertheless, he can't be found on
> the tips of the hundred weeds. Kuei Shan's answer covers
> heaven and earth.

COMMENTARY

The answers of these three men (to Pai Chang's question) are
all different from each other. There's (Kuei Shan's) towering up
like a thousand-fathom wall; there's (Wu Feng's) shining and
functioning at the same time; and there's (Yun Yen's) who
can't even save himself.

"'Please, Teacher, you speak instead.'" Immediately in this
one line Hsueh Tou has displayed his device. He goes farther
into it and presses ever so lightly to make it easy for people to
see by saying, "The tiger's head sprouts horns as he emerges
from the wild weeds." Kuei Shan's answer seems to be placing
horns on the head of a ferocious tiger—is there any way to
approach it?

Haven't you heard? A monk asked Lo Shan, "How is it when
they are born together and die together?" Shan said, "Like an
ox without horns." The monk asked, "How is it when they are
born together but don't die together?" Shan said, "Like a tiger
wearing horns."

Though Hsueh Tou has completed the verse in one couplet,
he has ample talent to turn around and change. He goes on and
says, "On the ten continents spring ends and the flowers fade

and wither." On the ocean there are ten continents where one hundred years make one spring. Hsueh Tou's words have graceful elegance, turning freely with great ease. When the spring is over, hundreds of thousands of myriad flowers fade and wither all at once. Only the coral tree forest doesn't fade and wither— it takes the light of the sun and reflects it back and forth (among the branches). At just such a time it is amazing indeed! Hsueh Tou uses this to illuminate Kuei Shan's saying, "Please, Teacher, you speak instead."

Wu Feng's Shut Up, Teacher

CASE

Pai Chang also asked Wu Feng, "With your throat, mouth, and lips shut, how will you speak?"[1]

Feng said, "Teacher, you too should shut up."[2]

Chang said, "Where there's no one, I shade my eyes with my hand and gaze out towards you."[3]

NOTES

1. Hahaha! The arrow has gone past Korea.
2. He captures the banner and carries off the drum. With a single phrase he cuts off the flow and puts to rest myriad impulses.
3. Where the land is broad and the population sparse, those met with are few.

COMMENTARY

Kuei Shan held fast to his territory—Wu Feng cut off the myriad streams. For this bit one must be a fellow who takes it up directly, like a head-on clash in the front lines. There's no room for hesitation. Wu Feng functions directly and immediately: (his reply) is urgent and swift, perilous and steep. He's not like Kuei Shan who is so relaxed and easy-going and exuberant.

Followers of Ch'an these days just move under the shelf, unable to go beyond him. Thus it is said, "If you want to attain Intimacy, don't ask with questions."

Wu Feng's answer cut him off immediately; undeniably it was fast and brilliant. Pai Chang said, "Where there's no one, I shade my eyes with my hand and gaze out towards you." But say, is this approving of Wu Feng or not? Is it killing or bringing to life? Seeing him turn so smoothly, Pai Chang just was giving him a check.

Hsueh Tou's verse says:

VERSE

"Teacher, you too should shut up."
> Already present before the words. It cuts off the myriad streams.

Observe Wu Feng's strategy on the dragon and snake battle
*   lines—*
> It takes the golden drum and serrated banner (of a great general) to be able to do this. He's fully equipped: he's an expert accustomed to battle.

He makes people think of General Li Kuang.
> There aren't many with such marvelous skill. With his horse and spear (he covers) a thousand miles, ten thousand miles, and (defeats) a thousand men, ten thousand men.

Over the ten-thousand-mile horizon a single kingfisher hawk
*   soars.*
> Does everyone see? But say, where does it alight? On target. I'll hit saying, "It's flown past."

COMMENTARY

"'Teacher, you too should shut up.'" In one line Hsueh Tou gives a push and says, "Observe his strategy on the dragon and snake battle lines." It is as though Wu Feng set out two battle lines to burst out and to burst in. He has the ability of a battle commander, unrestrained in all directions. A man with a grand strategy is free to appear and disappear with his horse and spear up on the dragon and snake battle lines. How would you be able to surround him? If you're not this kind of person, how will you know that there is this kind of strategy?

In all these three verses (70, 71, and 72) of Hsueh Tou's, what he describes within them is like this, like Li Kuang's miraculous arrows.[a] "Over the ten-thousand-mile horizon a single kingfisher hawk soars." That one arrow fells one eagle is certain: there's no more (chance of) escape. In Hsueh Tou's verse, Pai Chang's question is like a kingfisher hawk—Wu Feng's answer is like an arrow. I have been so occupied with praising Wu Feng that without realizing it my whole body has been immersed in mud and water.

TRANSLATORS' NOTES

a. A renowned archer and great general, Li Kuang had a long career fighting the Huns on the northern frontiers for the Western Han Dynasty in the middle of the second century B.C. See the commentary to the verse in case 4.

Pai Chang Questions Yun Yen

CASE

Pai Chang also asked Yun Yen, "With your throat, mouth, and lips shut, how will you speak?"[1]

Yen said, "Teacher, do you have (any way to speak) or not?"[2]

Chang said, "I have lost my descendants."[3]

NOTES

1. "Come out of your hole, frog." What is he saying?
2. Sticking to his skin, clinging to his bones. Mud and water is streaming off him. Ahead he doesn't reach the village, behind he doesn't get to the shop.
3. Obviously with an answer like this, half is in front and half is left behind.

COMMENTARY

Yun Yen was an attendant for twenty years at Pai Chang. Later he went along with Tao Wu to Yao Shan. Shan asked him, "When you were in Pai Chang's congregation, what was your purpose?" Yen said, "To escape birth and death." Shan said, "Have you escaped yet or not?" Yen said, "There's no birth and death for this one." Shan said, "Twenty years at Pai Chang and your force of habit still hasn't been cleared away yet." Yen took his leave and went to see Nan Ch'uan. Later he returned to Yao Shan and at last understood and was enlightened.

Look how the ancient man Yun Yen studied and investigated for twenty years and still was half green and half yellow (unripe). He stuck to his skin and clung to his bones, and couldn't break through. He was indeed this way; in fact, ahead he didn't reach the village, behind he didn't get to the shop. Haven't you heard it said:

If your words do not leave the old clichés,
How will you be able to get out of what covers and
  binds you?
White clouds lie athwart the valley mouth,
Making so many people miss the source.

In the Ts'ao Tung tradition this is called "transgression." Thus they say, "Throw open the well-guarded phoenix tower but avoid transgressing (the prohibition against saying) the present emperor's name." Hence it is said, "To attain it is first necessary to pass beyond the forest of brambles. If you do not pass beyond it, then from beginning to end you will get stuck in subtleties without being able to cut them off."

As I just said, "Ahead he didn't reach his village, behind he didn't get to his shop." Yun Yen just went to test the other man's depths. When Pai Chang saw him acting like this, he immediately held him and struck him dead.

Hsueh Tou's verse says:

VERSE

"Teacher, do you have (any way to speak) or not?"
  The case is perfectly manifest. Yun Yen was following the waves, pursuing the ripples, mixing with mud, mingling with water.

The golden-haired lion is not crouching on the ground.
  Obviously. What's the use? Too bad!

Two by two, three by three, travelling the old road—
  "With your throat, mouth, and lips shut, how will you speak?" Turn around and show some spirit! Though it was right under his feet, he missed it.

On Ta Hsiung Mountain Pai Chang snapped his fingers in
  vain.[a]
  Once dead Yun Yen did not come back to life again. Too bad! Too sad! Hsueh Tou adds more grief to his cry of woe.

COMMENTARY

" 'Teacher, do you have (any way to speak) or not?' / The golden-haired lion is not crouching on the ground." Hsueh Tou concludes the case on the basis of the facts. Yun Yen is indeed one, but this golden-haired lion nevertheless is not crouching on the ground (ready to spring). When a lion captures its prey, it conceals its teeth, hides its claws, and crouches on the ground to rear back (and leap). Whether the prey is large or small, a lion always uses his whole power, wanting to complete his deed.

When Yun Yen said, "Teacher, do you have (any way to speak) or not?" he was just travelling on his former road. That's why Hsueh Tou says that Pai Chang snapped his fingers in vain on Ta Hsiung Mountain.

TRANSLATORS' NOTES

a.   One snaps one's fingers at someone to make him wake up.

Ma Tsu's Permutations of Assertion and Denial

POINTER

In explaining the Dharma, there is neither explanation nor teaching; in listening to the Dharma, there is neither hearing nor attainment. Since explanation neither explains nor teaches, how can it compare to not explaining? Since listening neither hears nor attains, how can it compare to not listening? Still, no explaining and no listening still amount to something.

As for all of you right here, listening to me explain here, how will you avoid this mistake? For those with the eye to pass through the barrier, as a test, I'm citing this old case: look!

CASE

A monk asked Grand Master Ma, "Please, Teacher, going beyond the permutations of assertion and denial, directly point out to me the meaning of the coming from the West."[1]

Master Ma said, "I'm tired today and can't explain for you. Go ask Chih Tsang."[2]

When the monk asked Chih Tsang,[3] Tsang said, "Why didn't you ask the Teacher?"[4] The monk said, "The Teacher had me come here to ask you."[5] Tsang said, "I have a headache today and can't explain for you. Go ask Elder Brother Hai."[6] When the monk asked Elder Brother Hai (Pai Chang),[7] Hai said, "At this point, after all, I don't understand."[8]

When the monk related this to Grand Master Ma,[9] Master Ma said, "Tsang's head is white, Hai's head is black."[10]

NOTES

1. Where did he get this question from? Where did he get this news?
2. He retreats three paces. The monk has stumbled past without

realizing it. Ma hides his body but reveals his shadow. Undeniably this old fellow Ma has passed the buck to someone else.

3. He should have pressed Ma. He's stumbled past without realizing it.

4. The scorched-tail tiger has come out of the weeds. What is he saying? In fact, the monk is binding himself with straw ropes— he's totally dead.

5. He's at the disposal of someone else. The first arrow was still light, but the second arrow is deep.

6. It seems that the eighty-four men of knowledge (produced by Ma Tsu) all suffer from this kind of sickness.

7. Again the monk passes it to someone else. Clutching the loot, he cries out that he's been wronged.

8. He doesn't make a fuss. At any rate, the obscurity extends endlessly, forever and ever.

9. Despite everything, this monk does have a little eyesight.

10. In the heart of the realm, the emperor commands; outside the passes, the generals give orders.

COMMENTARY

In the old days when I studied with Chen Chueh in Ch'eng Tu (in Szechuan), Chueh said of this case, "You just need to look at Ma Tsu's first line and you will naturally understand all at once." Tell me, did this monk understand when he asked, or did he ask not understanding? This question of his is undeniably profound and far-reaching.

As for going beyond the permutations of assertion and denial, the four basic propositions are: 'it exists,' 'it doesn't exist,' 'it neither exist nor doesn't exist,' and 'it both exists and doesn't exist.' When you depart from these four propositions, you cut off their hundred negations. But if you just occupy yourself making up theories, you won't recognize the point of the story—you'll be looking for your head without seeing it.

If it had been me, I'd have waited until Ma Tsu had spoken, then unrolled my mat and bowed three times, to see how he would have responded. If I had been Ma Tsu at that time, when I saw this monk come up and ask, "Please, Teacher, going beyond the permutations of affirmation and denial, directly point out to me the meaning of the coming from the West," I would have brought my staff down across his back and driven him out with blows, to see if he would awaken or not.

Grand Master Ma just created complications for him. When this fellow was right in front of it and stumbled past missing it, Ma Tsu still directed him to go ask Chih Tsang. The monk really didn't know that Grand Master Ma profoundly discerns oncoming winds. The monk went in ignorance to ask Chih Tsang. Tsang said, "Why didn't you ask the Teacher?" The monk said, "The Teacher had me come here to ask you." Watch this bit of his: when pressed, he immediately turns without wasting any more time. Chih Tsang said, "I have a headache today and can't explain for you. Go ask Elder Brother Hai."

This monk went to ask Elder Brother Hai, who said, "At this point, after all, I don't understand." But say, why did one man say he had a headache and one man say he didn't understand? In the end, what's what? This monk then came back and related this to Grand Master Ma. The Master said, "Tsang's head is white, Hai's head is black."

If you figure this by way of intellectual interpretation, then you would say that they were fooling the monk. Some say that is was all just buck-passing. Some say that all three knew the monk's question, and therefore they didn't answer. All such interpretations amount to clapping your hands over your eyes and putting poison into the excellent-flavored pure ghee of the Ancients.

Thus Ma Tsu said (to Layman P'ang), "When you swallow all the water in West River in one gulp, then I'll explain to you." This is the same as the present case. If you can understand "Tsang's head is white, Hai's head is black," then you can understand this talk about West River's water.

This monk took his load of confusion and exchanged it for uneasiness: he went on troubling these three adepts, making them enter the mud and water. In the end this monk didn't catch a glimpse of it. Although it was like this throughout, nevertheless these three masters of our school were exposed by a board-carrying fellow.

People these days just go to the words to make their living. They say that white refers to merging in brightness, while black refers to merging in darkness. Just occupying themselves with pursuing their calculations, such people are far from knowing that the ancient Ma Tsu cuts off their intellectual faculties with a single line. You must go to the true lifeline and look for yourself before you can gain firm accord. Therefore Ma Tsu said, "With the last word you finally get to the impenetrable barrier." If you cut off the essential crossing place, you don't let profane or holy pass. If you discuss this matter, it's like having a sword pressing against your forehead—hesitate and you lose your body and your life. Again, it's said, "It's like hurling a sword into the sky—it's not a question of whether it reaches or not." Just go to the place of glistening clarity to understand.

Haven't you heard of the Ancients saying "You tub of lacquer!" or "Wild fox spirit!" or "Blind man!"? Tell me, is this the same as, or different from, a blow or a shout? If you know that the myriad differences and distinctions are all one, then naturally you will be able to take on opponents on all sides. Do you want to understand "Tsang's head is white, Hai's head is black"? My late teacher Wu Tsu said, "Mr. Dustsweeper."

Hsueh Tou's verse says:

VERSE

"Tsang's head is white, Hai's head is black."
　　Half closed, half open. One hand lifts up, one hand presses down. The sound of gold bells, the flourish of jewel chimes.

Clear-eyed patchrobed monks cannot understand.
　　Go travel for thirty more years. It ends with your nostrils being pierced by someone else. Because of this, my mouth seems to be in a frown.

The Colt has trampled everyone on earth to death—
　　Among all the monasteries, only this old fellow Ma could do this. Bring this old fellow out!

Lin Chi isn't yet a thief who can steal in broad daylight.
　　A leper drags along his companions. Even though Ma Tsu and Lin Chi are experts, they've been caught by another person, Hsueh Tou.

Going beyond the four propositions and cutting off their
    hundred negations—
    What is he saying? You too must check into this and see
    for yourself. "Poppa" resembles "daddy."
Among gods and humans only I know.
    Why use "I"? I'll snatch away your staff. If there's no self
    and no others, no gain and no loss, what will you use to
    know?

COMMENTARY

"'Tsang's head is white, Hai's head is black.'" But say, what
does this mean? The world's patchrobed monks can't leap clear
of this little bit. Look at how well Hsueh Tou closes up tight at
the end: he says that even if you're a clear-eyed patchrobed
monk you still won't be able to understand. This bit of news is
called the hidden secret of the spiritual immortals which is not
passed on from father to son. After old Shakyamuni had
preached the teachings of his entire lifetime, at the end he
specially transmitted the mind seal. It is called the Diamond
King's jewel sword;[a] it is called the Rank of the Correct.[b] Such
complications were a matter that couldn't be avoided—(with
them) the Ancients showed a little of their sharp point. If you
are a person who can pass through, then you will pierce and
penetrate to attain the great independence. If you can't pass
through, then as before there is no place for you to awaken and
enter, and the more you talk the farther away you are.

"The Colt has trampled everyone on earth to death." Back in
India Prajnatara prophesied to Bodhidharma (of Ma Tsu) saying,
"Though China is vast, there is no other road: it will run in the
footsteps of your descendants. A golden rooster will know how
to take a grain of millet in his beak and offer sustenance to the
arhats of the ten directions."[c] In addition, the Sixth Patriarch
said to (Ma Tsu's teacher) Master Jang, "Hereafter the Buddha
Dharma will go forth from you. In the future you will produce a
colt who will trample everyone on earth to death." After this
he did spread the teaching over the whole country as the
Dharma successor in Kiangsi—at the time he was called Ma

Tsu. Thus both Bodhidharma and the Sixth Patriarch predicted Ma Tsu in advance. Look how his way of doing things was, as it turned out, special—he just said, "Tsang's head is white, Hai's head is black." This is where to see how he tramples everyone on earth to death. A thousand men, ten thousand men can't bite through this one line about black and white.

"Lin Chi isn't yet a thief who can steal in broad daylight." One day Lin Chi taught his assembly saying, "In this red lump of flesh there is a true man without station. He's constantly going in and out through all of your senses. Those who haven't yet experienced this—look! look!" At the time there was a monk who came forward and asked, "What is the true man without station?" Lin Chi came down from the meditation platform and grabbed the monk tightly saying, "Speak! Speak!" The monk was speechless. Lin Chi pushed him away and said, "The true man without station—what a dry piece of shit he is!" Later Hsueh Feng heard of this and said, "Lin Chi greatly resembles a thief who steals in broad daylight."

Hsueh Tou wants to meet that Lin Chi, but in observing Ma Tsu's active edge, it is certainly superior to Lin Chi's. Ma Tsu is truly a thief who steals in broad daylight; Lin Chi is not yet one. Hsueh Tou has pierced them both at once.

Turning to versify this monk, Hsueh Tou says, "Going beyond the four propositions and cutting off their hundred negations—/Among gods and humans only I know." But don't go into the ghost cave to make your living! An Ancient said, "The question is in the answer, the answer is in the question." This monk was already extraordinary—how will you be able to go beyond the four propositions and cut off their hundred negations? Hsueh Tou says, "Only I know this matter." Even the Buddhas of past, present, and future cannot catch sight of it. Since each one must know for himself alone, what are all of you looking for when you keep on coming up here (to listen to me)?

Chen Ju of Ta Kuei commented, "This monk asking this way and Ma Tsu answering this way went beyond the permutations of assertion and denial. Chih Tsang and Elder Brother Hai didn't realize it at all."

Want to understand? Haven't you heard it said?—"The Colt has trampled everyone on earth to death."

TRANSLATORS' NOTES

a. The Diamond King's jewel sword is a symbol of *prajna*, transcendent wisdom.

b. The Rank of the Correct symbolizes emptiness, *nirvana;* see the appendix on the devices of Tung Shan.

c. Prajnatara was Bodhidharma's teacher, the Twenty-Seventh Indian Patriarch. "There is no other road" refers to Ma Tsu, whose Dharma name was Tao I, "The Path is one." "A golden rooster" refers to Ma Tsu's teacher, Master Huai Jang of Nan Yueh, a man from Chin Chou ("Gold Prefecture"); like a rooster who naturally knows how to crow at the right time, Huai Jang knew when to appear in the world to cause the Dharma to flourish. The "grain of millet" means the specially transmitted mind seal. The colt in Hsueh Tou's verse and in the Sixth Patriarch's prediction to Huai Jang, of course, means Ma Tsu: in Chinese, "Ma" means horse.

Chin Niu's Rice Pail

POINTER

Wielding a sharp sword horizontally, he cuts off the nest of trailing vines in front of his point. Hanging a clear mirror on high, he brings forth Vairocana's seal within a phrase. Where one's state is secure within, one wears clothes and eats food. Where spiritual powers wander at play, how can one linger? Have you fully mastered it? Look at what's written below:

CASE

Every day at mealtime, Master Chin Niu would personally take the rice pail and do a dance in front of the monks' hall: laughing aloud, he would say, "Bodhisattvas, come eat!"[1]

Hsueh Tou said, "Though he acted like this, Chin Niu was not good-hearted."[2]

A monk asked Ch'ang Ch'ing, "When the man of old said, 'Bodhisattvas, come eat!' what was his meaning?"[3] Ch'ing said, "Much like joyful praise on the occasion of a meal."[4]

NOTES

1. "You may play with the fishing line as you will—without disturbing the clear waves, its meaning is naturally distinct." He applies pure ghee and poison at the same time—and he's right! Jewels and gems he arrays all at once, but what can he do?—those he meets with are few.
2. This is a thief recognizing a thief, a spirit recognizing a spirit. If someone comes to talk of right and wrong, then he's a right and wrong person.
3. Indeed, anyone would have doubts about this. From the beginning, he hasn't known where Chin Niu is at. What will Ch'ang Ch'ing say?

4. He sizes up the audience to give his order, and wraps up the case on the basis of the facts.

COMMENTARY

Chin Niu was a venerable adept descended from Ma Tsu. Every day at mealtime he would personally take the rice pail and do a dance in front of the monks' hall: laughing aloud, he would say, "Bodhisattvas, come eat!" He did this for twenty years. Tell me, where was his intent? Was he just summoning the others to eat? He always struck the (wooden) fish and beat the drum (for mealtimes) and also personally announced it. So what further need was there for him to take the rice pail and do so many tricks? Wasn't he crazy? Wasn't he "expounding by design"? If he was expounding this matter, why didn't he mount the jewel flower throne to "knock on the seat and hold up the whisk"? Why did he need to act like this?

People today are far from knowing that the Ancients' meaning was outside of words. Why not then take a brief look at the stated purpose for the Patriarchal Teacher's first coming here? What was it? It was clearly explained: for a separate transmission outside the verbal teachings, to transmit individually the mind seal. The ancient man Chin Niu's expedient methods too were just to make you directly receive this. Later people would vainly calculate on their own and say, "Why so many concerns? When cold, turn toward the fire; when hot, take advantage of the cool shade; when hungry, eat; when tired, get some sleep." If we interpreted meanings this way, on the basis of ordinary feelings, to explain and comment, then the whole school of Bodhidharma would have been wiped off the face of the earth. Don't you realize that twenty-four hours a day, from moment to moment, the Ancients never gave up wanting to understand This Matter?

Hsueh Tou said, "Though he acted like this, Chin Niu was not good-hearted." Many people misunderstand this line. That which is called the supreme flavor of pure ghee is converted, on encountering such people, into poison. Since Chin Niu descended into the weeds to help people, why did Hsueh Tou say that he wasn't good-hearted? Why did he talk this way? Patch-robed monks must have living potential to begin to understand this.

People today don't get to the Ancient's realm—they just say, "What mind is there to see? What Buddha is there?" If you construct such views you have destroyed the old adept, Chin Niu. It takes thorough observation to begin to understand. If today and tomorrow you go on with such facile explanations, you'll never be finished.

Later when Ch'ang Ch'ing had gone up to his seat, a monk asked, "When the ancient man said, 'Bodhisattvas, come eat!' what was his meaning?" Ch'ing said, "Much like joyful praise on the occasion of a meal." The honored worthy Ch'ang Ch'ing was extremely compassionate—he leaked and tarried quite a bit. In truth it was "joyful praise on the occasion of a meal." But you tell me, rejoicing over what?

Look at Hsueh Tou's verse which says:

VERSE

Laughing aloud in the shadow of the white clouds,
      In his laugh, there's a knife. Why the enthusiasm? The world's patchrobed monks don't know where he comes down.
He lifts it up with both hands to give to them.
      How can there be such things? Better not slander Chin Niu! Can it be called a rice pail? If you are a legitimate patchrobed monk in your own right, you don't eat this kind of food.
If they were sons of the golden-haired lion,
      They must first be beyond patterns. I'll allow that they had eyes, but I only fear that their eyes were not true.
They would have seen the deception from three thousand
      miles away.
      It wasn't worth half a cent. A scene of leaking and tarrying. Where was the deception? Blind men!

COMMENTARY

"Laughing aloud in the shadow of the white clouds." Ch'ang Ch'ing says, "Joyful praise on the occasion of a meal." Hsueh

Tou says, "He lifts it up with both hands to give to them." But say, was he just giving them food to eat, or do you think that there must have been something special besides? If you can know the true point here, then you're a son of the golden-haired lion. If they had been sons of the golden-haired lion, then there would have been no more need for Chin Niu to take the rice pail, do a dance, and laugh aloud—in fact they would have known his mistake immediately from three thousand miles away.

An Ancient said, "Perceive before the act and you won't have to use the least bit of effort." Thus patchrobed monks must always function outside of patterns before they can be called genuine Masters of our school. If they just base themselves on words and speech, they won't avoid leaking and tarrying in indulgent attachments.

Wu Chiu's Unjust Beating

POINTER

The subtle point, the jewel sword, perpetually revealed, present in front of us. It can kill people and it can bring people life. It's there and it's here, gaining and losing together with us. If you want to pick it up, you're free to pick it up; if you want to put it down, you're free to put it down.

But say, what's it like when not falling into guest and host, when interchanging without getting stuck? To test, I'm citing this old case: look!

CASE

A monk came to Wu Chiu from the congregation of the Master of Ting Chou. Wu Chiu asked, "How does Ting Chou's Dharma Path compare to here?"[1] The monk said, "It's not different."[2] Chiu said, "If it's not different, then you should go back there," and then hit him.[3] The monk said, "There are eyes on the staff: you shouldn't carelessly hit people."[4] Chiu said, "Today I've hit one," and hit him again three times.[5] The monk thereupon went out.[6]

Chiu said, "All along there's been someone receiving an unjust beating."[7] The monk turned around and said, "What can I do? The handle is in your hands, Teacher."[8] Chiu said, "If you want, I'll turn it over to you."[9] The monk came up to Chiu, grabbed the staff out of his hands, and hit him three times.[10] Chiu said, "An unjust beating, an unjust beating!"[11] The monk said, "There's someone receiving it."[12]

Chiu said, "I hit this fellow carelessly."[13] Immediately the monk bowed.[14] Chiu said, "Yet you act this way."[15] The monk laughed loudly and went out.[16] Chiu said, "That's all it comes to, that's all it comes to."[17]

NOTES

1. There's an echo in his words. He must distinguish shallow from deep. (The question is like) a probing pole, a reed shade. He's really deceiving the man!
2. Among the dead men there's a live one. One or a half. ("Not different") is the same as an iron spike. He's treading upon the ground of reality.
3. Obviously. The correct imperative must be carried out.
4. Only this adept could do this. After all, he's a lion cub.
5. What one is he talking about? (Why not hit) a thousand, ten thousand?
6. All along the monk's been a man of our house. In fact he has been wronged. He just sees his opportunity and goes.
7. A mute eating a bitter melon. Chiu both lets go and gathers in. What good is someone who turns back around when hit?
8. It's this way three hundred and sixty-five days a year. After all he is a clever patchrobed monk.
9. Who knows which of them is the prince and which is the minister? Chiu dares to lie down in the tiger's mouth. He really doesn't know good from evil.
10. Here again, only an adept Ch'an traveller could do this. Guest and host interchange, releasing or capturing according to the occasion.
11. Check! Why is this old fellow in such a rush?
12. Haha! How many handles are now in this monk's hands?
13. It doesn't come down on either side. Who knows who he is?
14. Only one who doesn't flinch when faced with danger is a man of power.
15. Check!
16. An adept Ch'an traveller naturally has (such ability). A fierce tiger must have a pure wind following him. Now we know that he finished the beginning and finished the end. No one on earth can get a grasp on him.
17. Too bad he let the monk go. Why didn't he bring his staff down across his back? Where do you think the monk went?

COMMENTARY

A monk came to Wu Chiu from the congregation of the Master of Ting Chou. Chiu was also an adept. If here all of you people can realize that there was a single exit and a single entry for these two men, then a thousand or ten thousand is in fact just one. It is so, whether acting as host or as guest: in the end the two men merge together into one agent for one session of careful investigation. Whether as guest or host, whether asking or answering, from beginning to end both were adepts.

Look at Wu Chiu questioning this monk: "How does Ting Chou's Dharma Path compare to here?" The monk immediately said, "It's not different." At the time, if it hadn't been Wu Chiu, it would have been hard to cope with this monk. Chiu said, "If it's not different, then you should go back there," and then hit him. But what could he do? This monk was an adept and immediately said, "There are eyes on the staff: you shouldn't carelessly hit people." Chiu carried out the imperative thoroughly saying, "Today I've hit one," and hitting him again three more times. At this the monk went out. Observe how the two of them revolved so smoothly—both were adepts. To understand this affair it is necessary to distinguish initiate from lay, and tell right from wrong. Though this monk went out, the case was still not finished.

From beginning to end Wu Chiu wanted to test this monk's reality, to see how he was. But this monk had barred the door, so Chiu hadn't yet seen him. Then Wu Chiu said, "All along there's been someone receiving an unjust beating." This monk wanted to turn around and show some life, yet he didn't struggle with Wu Chiu, but turned around most easily and said, "What can I do? The handle is in your hands, Teacher." Being a Master of our school with an eye on his forehead, Wu Chiu dared to lay his body down in the fierce tiger's mouth and say, "If you want, I'll turn it over to you."

This monk was a fellow with a talisman under his arm. As it is said, "To see what is right and not do it is lack of bravery." Without hesitating any longer, the monk came up to Wu Chiu, grabbed the staff out of his hands, and hit him three times. When Chiu said, "An unjust beating, an unjust beating!" tell me, what did he mean? Before, Chiu said, "All along there's been someone receiving an unjust beating." But when the monk hit him he said, "An unjust beating, an unjust beating!" When the monk said, "There's someone receiving it," Chiu said, "I hit this fellow carelessly." Chiu said before that he had hit a person carelessly. Afterwards, when he had taken a beating himself, why did he also say, "I hit this fellow carelessly"? If it hadn't been for this monk's independent resurgence, he couldn't have been able to handle Wu Chiu.

Then the monk bowed. This bow was extremely poisonous—it wasn't good-hearted. If it hadn't been Wu Chiu, he wouldn't have been able to see through this monk. Wu Chiu said to him, "Yet you act this way." The monk laughed loudly and went out. Wu Chiu said, "That's all it comes to, that's all it comes to."

Observe how all through the meeting of these adepts, guest and host are distinctly clear. Though cut off, they can still continue. In fact this is just an action of interchanging. Yet when they get here, they do not say that there is an interchange. Since these ancient men were beyond defiling feelings and conceptual thinking, neither spoke of gain or loss. Though it was a single session of talk, the two men were both leaping with life, and both had the needle and thread of our blood line. If you can see here, you too will be perfectly clear twenty-four hours a day.

When the monk (first) went out, this was both sides letting go. What happened after that was both sides gathering in. This is called interchanging. Hsueh Tou makes his verse just this way:

VERSE

To summon is easy—
> Everyone on earth doubts this. Rancid meat attracts flies. None of the world's patchrobed monks know where this comes down.

To send away is hard.
> Getting rid of them thoroughly (is hard). Mirages appear over the sea.

Observe carefully the interchange of action points.
> One exit, one entry—both are adepts. Two men hold a single staff. But say, whose side is it on?

The rock of ages though solid can still crumble—
> How will you handle the golden hammer up his sleeve? The thousand sages haven't transmitted it.

When they stand in its depths the ocean must dry up.
    Where will this be arranged? There are eyes on the staff.
    I'll only allow that they have attained intimately.

Old Wu Chiu! Old Wu Chiu!
    What a pity that this old fellow doesn't know good from
    evil.

How many kinds?
    He's another fellow with no reasons (for what he does).
    Hundreds, thousands, myriads of miles.

Indeed he had no reason for giving him the handle.
    Already so before the words. Wu Chiu's life was hanging
    by a thread. He deserves thirty blows. But say, where was
    his fault?

COMMENTARY

"To summon is easy—to send away is hard." It's all falling into
the weeds. With his excessive compassion, Hsueh Tou would
often say, "Calling snakes is easy; sending snakes away is
hard." Right now if I were to take a (dried and hollow) gourd
and blow through it, it would be easy to summon snakes, but
when I wanted to send them away it would be hard. Similarly,
it's easy to give one's staff to someone else, but to take it back
from him and send him away is hard. You must have your own
ability—only then will you be able to send him away.

Wu Chiu was an adept with the skill to call snakes and also
the ability to send snakes away. This monk wasn't asleep
either. When Wu Chiu asked, "How does Ting Chou's Dharma
Path compare to here?"—this was calling him. When Wu Chiu
then hit him, this was sending him away. When the monk said,
"There are eyes on the staff: you shouldn't hit people
carelessly"—this is the summoning transferred over to the
monk's side. When Wu Chiu said, "If you want, I'll turn it over
to you," and the monk then came up to Chiu, grabbed the staff
out of his hands, and hit him three times—this was the monk
sending him away. As for the monk laughing loudly and going
out, and Wu Chiu saying, "That's all it comes to"—this clearly
is each sending the other away appropriately.

Observe how these two exchanged action points, spinning
with perfect continuity, fusing into one whole. From beginning

to end, guest and host are clearly distinct. Sometimes, though, host acts as guest and sometimes guest acts as host. Even Hsueh Tou cannot praise this enough. Thus he speaks of the act of interchange and has you people observe it carefully. "The rock of ages though solid can still crumble." He speaks of this "rock of ages": it's 84,000 leagues wide and 84,000 leagues thick.[a] Every five hundred years a god comes down and brushes across it with a gossamer cloth, then departs for another five hundred years. The brushing continues like this until it wears the rock away—this makes one age called the "light cloth brushing across the rock" age. Hsueh Tou says, "The rock of ages though solid can still crumble." Though the rock is strong and solid, still it can be worn away to nothing. But the action point of these two men can never be obliterated over the ages.

"When they stand in its depths the ocean must dry up." Even the ocean, with its vast swelling billows flooding the skies, even the very ocean would inevitably dry up utterly if you have these two men stand within it. At this point Hsueh Tou has completed his verse all at once.

At the end he goes on to say, "Old Wu Chiu! Old Wu Chiu!/How many kinds?" Sometimes catching, sometimes letting go; sometimes killing, sometimes giving life—in the end, how many kinds is this? "Indeed he had no reason for giving him the handle." This staff has been used by all the Buddhas of past, present, and future, and by the successive generations of Patriarchal Teachers, and by the Masters of our school, to pull out nails and extract pegs for people, to loosen what is stuck and untie what is bound. How can it be given over to someone else lightly? Hsueh Tou means that it should be used by oneself alone. Fortunately it happened that this monk then just opened up to him—if he had suddenly stirred up thunder over dry ground, we would have observed how Chiu met it. When Wu Chiu passed him the handle, wasn't this indeed without any reason?

TRANSLATORS' NOTES

a. Yojana is a unit of distance: a day's march by the king and his retinue in ancient India; maybe ten or twenty miles.

Tan Hsia's Have You Eaten Yet?

POINTER

Fine as rice powder, cold as icy frost, it blocks off heaven and earth and goes beyond light and dark. Observe it where it's low and there's extra; level it off where it's high and there's not enough. Holding fast and letting go are both here, but is there a way to appear or not? To test I'm citing this old case: look!

CASE

Tan Hsia asked a monk, "Where have you come from?"¹ The monk said, "From down the mountain."² Hsia said, "Have you eaten yet or not?"³ The monk said, "I have eaten."⁴ Hsia said, "Did the person who brought you the food to eat have eyes or not?"⁵ The monk was speechless.⁶

Ch'ang Ch'ing asked Pao Fu, "To give someone food to eat is ample requital of the debt of kindness: why wouldn't he have eyes?"⁷ Fu said, "Giver and receiver are both blind."⁸ Ch'ang Ch'ing said, "If they exhausted their activity, would they still turn out blind?"⁹ Fu said, "Can you say that I'm blind?"¹⁰

NOTES

1. It's truly impossible to have no place at all you've come from. If he wants to know where he's come from, it won't be hard.
2. He has put on his straw sandals and walked into your belly. It's just that you don't understand. There's an echo in his words, but he keeps it to himself. Is he yellow or green?
3. A second ladleful of foul water douses the monk. Why just the zero point of a scale? He wants to know the real truth.
4. As it turns out, he's collided with the pillar. After all, he's had his nostrils pierced by a bystander. From the beginning it's been an iron hammer head with no handle hole.

5. Although he is relying on his power to mystify the man, he is also wrapping up the case on the basis of the facts. At the time he deserved to have his meditation seat overturned. Why is there no reason for what he did?

6. After all, he couldn't run. If this monk had been an adept he would have said to him, "The same as your eyes, Teacher."

7. He's still only said half. Is it "throughout the body" or is it "all over the body"? One cut, two pieces. One hand lifts up, one hand presses down.

8. He acts according to the imperative. With one line he says it all. Such a man is rarely encountered.

9. What does he know of good and evil? He still isn't settled himself: what bowl is he looking for?

10. The two of them are both in the weeds. Fu has a dragon's head but a snake's tail. At the time when he said, "If they had exhausted their activity, would they still turn out blind?" I would have just said to him, "You're blind." Since they're both adepts, why is it that "ahead they didn't reach the village, behind they didn't get to the shop"?

COMMENTARY

"Tan Hsia" was Ch'an Master T'ien Jan of Tan Hsia in Teng Province of Honan—I don't know what locality he was from. At first he studied Confucianism, intending to go to Ch'ang-an to take part in the examinations for official posts. Then unexpectedly while he was staying over at a travellers' lodge, he dreamed that a white light filled the room. A diviner said, "This is an auspicious omen of understanding emptiness." There happened to be a Ch'an traveller there who asked him, "Good man, where are you going?" He said, "To be chosen to be an official." The Ch'an traveller said, "How can choosing an official career compare to choosing Buddhahood?" Tan Hsia asked, "What place should I go to to choose Buddhahood?" The Ch'an traveller said, "At the present time Grand Master Ma has appeared in the world in Kiangsi. This is the place to choose Buddhahood—you should go there, good man."

After this Tan Hsia went directly to Kiangsi. The moment he saw Grand Master Ma he lifted up the edge of his turban (to look at Ma). Master Ma observed him and said, "I am not your

Teacher—go to Shih T'ou's place in Nan Yueh." Tan Hsia hastened to Nan Yueh where he submitted to Shih T'ou with the same idea as before (at Ma Tsu's place). Shih T'ou told him to go to the stable, and Tan Hsia bowed in thanks. He entered the workmen's hall and worked along with the congregation for three years.

One day Shih T'ou announced to the assembly, "Tomorrow we're going to clear away the weeds in front of the Buddha's shrine." The next day everyone equipped himself with a hoe to cut down the weeds. Tan Hsia alone took a bowl, filled it with water, and washed his head; then he knelt in front of Master Shih T'ou. Shih T'ou saw this and laughed at him, then shaved his head for him. As Shih T'ou began to explain the precepts for him, Tan Hsia covered his ears and went out.

Then Tan Hsia headed for Kiangsi to call again on Ma Tsu. Before meeting with Ma Tsu to pay his respects, he went into the monks' hall and sat astride the neck of the holy statue (of Manjusri). At the time everybody became very perturbed and hurried to report this to Ma Tsu. Tsu personally went to the hall to have a look at him and said, "My son is so natural." Hsia immediately got down and bowed saying, "Thank you, Master, for giving me a Dharma name." Because of this he was called T'ien Jan (which means natural). This man of old Tan Hsia was naturally sharply outstanding like this. As it is said, "Choosing officialdom isn't as good as choosing Buddhahood." His sayings are recorded in the *Records of the Transmission of the Lamp*.

His words tower up like a thousand-fathom wall. Each and every line has the ability to pull out nails and extract pegs for people, like when he asked this monk, "Where have you come from?" The monk said, "From down the mountain," yet he didn't communicate where he had come from. It seemed that he had eyes and was going to reverse things and examine the host. If it hadn't been Tan Hsia, it would have been impossible to gather him in.

But Tan Hsia said, "Have you eaten yet or not?" At first he hadn't been able to see this monk at all, so this is the second attempt to examine him. The monk said, "I have eaten." From the beginning this confused and ignorant fellow hadn't understood. Hsia said, "Did the person who brought you the food to eat have eyes or not?" and the monk was speechless. Tan Hsia's meaning was, "What's the use of giving food to such a fellow as you?" If this monk had been a fellow (with eyes) he would have given Tan Hsia a poke to see what he would do. Nevertheless, Tan Hsia still didn't let him go, so the monk was (left standing there) blinking stupidly and speechless.

When Pao Fu and Ch'ang Ch'ing were together in Hsueh Feng's congregation, they would often bring up the public cases of the Ancients to discuss. Ch'ang Ch'ing asked Pao Fu, "To give someone food is ample requital of kindness: why wouldn't he have eyes?" He didn't have to inquire exhaustively into the facts of the case; he could take it all in using these words to pose his question. He wanted to test Pao Fu's truth. Pao Fu said, "Giver and receiver are both blind." How direct! Here he just discusses the immediate circumstances—inside his house Pao Fu has a way to assert himself.

When Ch'ang Ch'ing said, "If they had exhausted their activity, would they still turn out blind?" Pao Fu said, "Can you say that I'm blind?" Pao Fu meant, "I have such eyes to have said it all to you—are you still saying I'm blind?" Nevertheless, it's half closed and half open. At that time if it had been me, when he said, "If they had exhausted their activity, would they still turn out blind?" I would have just said to him, "You're blind." What a pity! If Pao Fu had uttered this one word "blind" at that time, he would have avoided so many of Hsueh Tou's complications. Hsueh Tou too just uses this idea to make his verse:

VERSE

(Ch'ang Ch'ing) exhausts his activity, (Pao Fu) doesn't become blind—
They've only said half. Each wanted to test the other. The words are still in our ears.

(Like) holding down an ox's head to make it eat grass.
They lose their money and incur punishment. Half south of the river, half north of the river. Without realizing it, they've run afoul of the point and cut their hands.

Twenty-eight and six Patriarchs—
If you have a rule, hold on to the rule. Hsueh Tou is dragging down the former sages; he doesn't just involve one man.

Their precious vessel is brought forth, but it turns out to be an error.
Everyone on earth beats his breast (in sorrow). Give me back my staff. They've dragged me down so that I can't even show my face.

The error is profound—
Extremely profound. The world's patchrobed monks cannot leap clear of it. But tell me, how profound?

There's no place to look for it.
Though it's right beneath your feet, it can't be found.

Gods and humans sink down together on dry land.
The world's patchrobed monks are all buried in one pit. Is there anyone alive? I let my move go. Heavens! Heavens!

COMMENTARY

"(Ch'ang Ch'ing) exhausts his activity, (Pao Fu) doesn't become blind." Ch'ang Ch'ing said, "If they exhausted their activity, would they still turn out blind?" Pao Fu said, "Can you say that I'm blind?" This was all like "Holding down an ox's head to make it eat grass." To get it right you must wait till he eats on his own: how can you push down an ox's head and make him eat? When Hsueh Tou versifies like this, naturally we can see Tan Hsia's meaning.

"Twenty-eight and six Patriarchs—/Their precious vessel is brought forth, but it turns out to be an error." Not only does Hsueh Tou drag down Ch'ang Ch'ing, but at the same time he buries the twenty-eight Patriarchs of India and the six Patriarchs of this country. In forty-nine years, old man Shakyamuni preached the whole great treasurehouse of the Teachings; at the end he only transmitted this precious vessel. Yung Chia said, "This is not an empty exhibition displaying form: it's the actual traces of the Tathagata's jewel staff." If you adopt Pao Fu's view, then even if you bring forth the precious vessel, it all turns out to be an error.

"The error is profound—/There's no place to look for it."
This can't be explained for you: just go sit quietly and inquire
into his lines and see. Since the error is profound, why then is
there no place to look for it? This is not a small mistake: he
takes the Great Affair of the Buddhas and Patriarchs and sub-
merges it entirely on dry land. Hence Hsueh Tou says, "Gods
and humans sink down together on dry land."

Yun Men's Cake

POINTER

Turning upwards, he can pierce the nostrils of everyone on earth, like a falcon catching a pigeon. Turning downwards, his own nostrils are in the hands of other people, like a turtle hiding in its shell.

Here if someone suddenly comes forth and says, "Fundamentally, there is no upwards and downwards—what use is turning?" I simply say to him, "I know that you are going inside the ghost cave to make your living."

But say, how will you distinguish initiate from naive? After a silence, Yuan Wu said, "If you have precepts, go by the precepts; if you have no precepts, go by the example."

CASE

A monk asked Yun Men, "What is talk that goes beyond Buddhas and Patriarchs?"[1] Men said, "Cake."[2]

NOTES

1. He opens up. Suddenly there's thunder over the parched earth. He presses.
2. The tongue is pressed against the roof of the mouth. It's gone by.

COMMENTARY

This monk asked Yun Men, "What is talk that goes beyond Buddhas and Patriarchs?" Men said, "Cake." Do you feel your hairs standing on end with the chill? Patchrobed monks have asked about Buddhas and asked about Patriarchs, asked about Ch'an and asked about Tao, asked about facing upwards and facing downwards—there's nothing more that can be asked, yet this one posed a question and asked about talk that goes beyond Buddhas and Patriarchs. Yun Men was an adept: thus, when the water rises, the boats ride high, and when there is much mud the Buddha-image is big. So he answered saying "Cake." It can be said that the Way is not carried out in vain, that his effort is not wasted.

Yun Men also taught the assembly saying, "Without any understanding, when you see people talking about the intent of the Patriarchal Teachers you immediately ask for theories of talk that goes beyond Buddhas and Patriarchs. But what do you call 'Buddhas,' what do you call 'Patriarchs,' that you immediately speak of talk that transcends Buddhas and Patriarchs? Then you ask about escape from the triple world, but you take hold of the triple world to see. What seeing, hearing, feeling, and knowing are there to hinder you? What phenomena of sound and form are there that you can be made to understand? What 'bowl' do you know how to use? On what basis do you entertain views of differentiations? Those ancient sages can't do anything for you, though they extend themselves to help living beings. Even if they say that the whole Body is entirely real, that in everything we see the Essence—this is ungraspable. When I say to you, 'In fact, what concerns are there?' this has already buried it." If you can understand this statement, then you can recognize the "Cake."

Wu Tsu said, "Donkey shit is like horse shit." This is what Yung Chia called "Going direct to the root source, as the Buddhas have sealed—picking through leaves and searching through twigs I cannot do." When you get to this point, if you want to attain Intimacy, don't ask with questions.

Observe how this monk asked, "What is talk that goes beyond Buddhas and Patriarchs?" and Yun Men said, "Cake." Does Yun Men know shame? Is he aware of indulging? There's a type of phoney person who says, "Yun Men saw the rabbit and released the hawk; thus he said 'Cake.'" If you take such a view, that "Cake" is talk that goes beyond Buddhas and Patriarchs, how can there be a living road? Don't understand it as cake and don't understand it as going beyond Buddhas and Patriarchs—this, then, is the living road. (Yun Men's "Cake") is the same as (Tung Shan's) "Three pounds of hemp" (Case 12) and (Ho Shan's) "Knowing how to beat the drum" (Case 44): though he just said "Cake," its reality is hard to see.

Later people often made up rationalizations and said, "Coarse words and subtle talk all come back to the primary truth." If you understand in this fashion, just go be a lecturer and spend your life collecting much knowledge and many interpretations. Followers of Ch'an these days say, "When you go beyond the Buddhas and Patriarchs you are trampling both Buddhas and Patriarchs underfoot—that's why Yun Men just said to him, 'Cake.'" Since it's "Cake," how does this explain going beyond the Buddhas and Patriarchs? Try to investigate thoroughly and see.

In the various places the verses about this case are extremely numerous, but they all go to the side of the question to make their comment. Hsueh Tou alone has versified it the best—naturally he's outstanding. The verse says:

VERSE

*Ch'an travellers asking about transcendent talk are especially
    numerous.*
    One after another they come forth and make up this kind
    of view, (numerous as) hemp or millet.
His gap opens—see it?
    Already open before the words. Hsueh Tou doesn't notice
    the smell of his own shit.
Even the cake stuffed in doesn't stop him.
    He's replaced your eyes with wooden beads.
Up till now there has been confusion all over the world.
    I'll draw a circle and say, "Haven't you been understand-
    ing this way?" What end is there to chewing over the
    words of others? The great earth is desolate, killing people
    with sadness, so I'll hit.

COMMENTARY

"Ch'an travellers asking about transcendent talk are especially numerous." Followers of Ch'an are especially fond of asking about this saying ("talk that goes beyond Buddhas and Patriarchs"). Haven't you heard? Yun Men said, "All of you carry

a staff across your shoulders and say, 'I am immersed in meditation, I am studying the Path,' and then go looking for a truth
that goes beyond the Buddhas and Patriarchs. But I ask you,
during the twenty-four hours of the day, when walking, standing, sitting, and lying down; when shitting and pissing among
the vermin in a roadside privy; when at the counter of the
butcher's stall in the market; is there still any truth that goes
beyond the Buddhas and Patriarchs? Let those who can speak of
it come forward. If there isn't anyone (who can), then don't stop
me from acting this way and that as I please." Then Yun Men
went down from his seat.

Some can no longer tell right from wrong—they draw a circle, adding mud to dirt, putting on chains while wearing
stocks. "His gap opens—see it?" What a big gap there is in this
monk posing his question! Yun Men saw it opening up in his
question, so he said "Cake" to block it up tight. But this monk
still wouldn't agree to stop—instead, he went on asking. Thus
Hsueh Tou says, "Even the cake stuffed in doesn't stop him."

"Up till now there has been confusion all over the world."
Followers of Ch'an these days just go to "Cake" to understand,
or else they go to "beyond Buddhas and Patriarchs" to make up
theories. Since it's not in these two places, in the end, where is
it? Thirty years from now, when I've exchanged my bones, I'll
tell you.

Sixteen Bodhisattvas Go In to Bathe

CASE

In olden times there were sixteen bodhisattvas.[1] When it was time for monks to wash, the bodhisattvas filed in to bathe.[2] Suddenly they awakened to the basis of water.[3] All of you Ch'an worthies, how will you understand their saying, "Subtle feeling reveals illumination,[4] and we have achieved the station of sons of Buddha"?[5] To realize this you too must be extremely piercing and penetrating.[6]

NOTES

1. What's the use of forming a crowd? This bunch of idiots!
2. They've collided with the pillar. Why such lacquer tubs?
3. Suddenly their heads are soaked with foul water.
4. It's no longer anyone else's business. How will you understand them? "Having knocked it down, it's nothing else."
5. Here the world's patchrobed monks seek but cannot find. Why two heads, three faces?
6. One blow with the staff, one welt. Better not turn your back on me! You're colliding with it, you're bumping into it. Have you ever seen Te Shan and Lin Chi?

COMMENTARY

At the Surangama Assembly, Bhadrapala and the sixteen bodhisattvas all practiced pure conduct and each related the basis on which he had experienced the Dharma gate of perfect pervasiveness. This is numbered as one among twenty-five (kinds of) perfect pervasiveness. (They related that) when it was time for monks to bathe they had filed in to bathe and suddenly awakened to the basis of water. Since they didn't wash off the dirt, and they didn't wash their bodies, tell me, what did they wash? If you can understand, then, at peace within, you realize the absence of anything existing. Then a thousand or ten thousand will no longer be able to get near you. As it is said, "Absence of attainment is true wisdom; if there is something which is attained, this is just semblance wisdom."

Haven't you heard? Bodhidharma said to the Second Patriarch, "Bring out your mind and I will pacify it for you." The Second Patriarch said, "When I search for my mind, I can't find it." This little bit here is the basic root of patchrobed monks' lives. There's no more need at all for so many complications: all that's needed is to speak of suddenly awakening to the basis of water, and you spontaneously understand properly.

Since they didn't wash off the dust, and they didn't wash their bodies, tell me, what did they awaken to? When you get to this realm, nothing at all is applicable—even the word "Buddha" must be avoided. They said, "Subtle feeling reveals illumination, and we have achieved the station of sons of Buddha." "Reveals" means "makes apparent." The subtle feeling is illumination. Once you awaken to the subtle feeling, then you achieve the station of sons of Buddha, that is, you are in the stage of Buddhahood.

People these days also go in to bathe, they also wash in water and feel it this way. Why then don't they awaken? They are all confused and obstructed by the objects of the senses: they stick to their skins and cling to their bones. That's why they can't wake up immediately then and there. Here, if there's nothing attained in washing or feeling or in the basis of water, then tell me, is this "Subtle feeling reveals illumination" or not? If here you can see directly, then this is "Subtle feeling reveals illumination, and we achieve the station of sons of Buddha." People these days feel too, but do they perceive its subtlety? Subtle feeling is not ordinary feeling and feeler, where contact is considered feeling and separation is not.

When Hsuan Sha was crossing the mountains and stubbed his toe (thereupon awakening), when Te Shan hits—isn't this subtle feeling? Although it is so, to realize this you must be extremely piercing and penetrating. If you just search on your body, what connection is there? If you are extremely piercing and penetrating, then what need is there to go in and wash? You will make the jewel king's realm appear on the tip of a hair and turn the great Dharma Wheel in every speck of dust. If you can penetrate in one place, then you penetrate a thousand places, ten thousand places all at once. Don't just hold onto a single nook or den—all places are the gates by which Avalokitesvara enters the truth.

For the Ancients too there was "awakening to the Path by hearing sounds, illuminating Mind by seeing forms." If a single man awakens, this is the reason. But why did the sixteen bodhisattvas awaken at the same time? Because the Ancients practiced together and experienced together, awakened together and understood together. Hsueh Tou picks up the meaning of their teaching to make people go to where "Subtle feeling reveals illumination" to understand. But Hsueh Tou goes beyond the eye of their teaching to let people avoid being trapped within the net of the teaching, half-drunk and half-sober. He wants to make people directly become clean, free, and unbound. The verse says:

VERSE

I only need one patchrobed monk who understands this matter—
There's one right here. I'll give him three thousand blows in the morning and eight hundred blows at night. Leap out of the unbreakable trap! Not even one is needed.

Stretch out your legs on the long-bench and lie down.
After all he's a sleepyhead. For eons he never discusses Ch'an.

In a dream you once spoke of awakening to perfect pervasiveness—
Already asleep, he goes on to speak of dreams. Yet I'll allow that he has seen it in dreams. Why the talking in his sleep?

Though you've washed in fragrant water, I'll spit right in your face.
Bah! He adds another layer of mud on top of the dirt. Don't come and shit on the clean ground!

COMMENTARY

"I only need one patchrobed monk who understands this matter." But say, understands what matter? Once they hear it mentioned, adept Ch'an travellers immediately go carry it out. It just takes one such patchrobed monk—what's the use of forming a crowd?

"Stretch out your legs on the long-bench and lie down." An Ancient said, "In clear illumination, there is no such thing as awakening. (The concept of) 'having awakened' turns around and deludes people. When you stretch out both feet and sleep, there's no false and there's no true—thus, there isn't a single concern in one's heart. When hungry, one eats; when tired, one sleeps."

Hsueh Tou means that if you speak of going in to wash and awakening to "Subtle feeling reveals illumination," from the standpoint of this kind of unconcerned patchrobed monk, this is just like speaking of a dream in a dream. That's why Hsueh Tou says, "In a dream you once spoke of awakening to perfect pervasiveness—Though you've washed in fragrant water, I'll spit right in your face." Though it seems like fragrant water, in fact it's foul water suddenly soaking your head. What "perfect pervasiveness" can you go on talking about? Hsueh Tou says that this sort of fellow quite rightly gets his face spattered with spit. I say that this is adding another layer of mud on top of dirt.

T'ou Tzu's All Sounds

POINTER

When his great function manifests before you it doesn't keep to patterns and rules. He captures you alive without exerting superfluous effort. But say, who has ever acted this way? To test I'm citing this old case: look!

CASE

A monk asked T'ou Tzu, "All sounds are the sounds of Buddha—right or wrong?"[1] T'ou Tzu said, "Right."[2] The monk said, "Teacher, doesn't your asshole make farting sounds?"[3] T'ou Tzu then hit him.[4]

Again the monk asked, "Coarse words or subtle talk, all returns to the primary meaning—right or wrong?"[5] T'ou Tzu said, "Right."[6] The monk said, "Can I call you an ass, Teacher?"[7] T'ou Tzu then hit him.[8]

NOTES

1. This monk too knows how to grab the tiger's whiskers. Crashing thunderclaps in a clear sky. He doesn't notice the bad smell of his own shit.
2. He's utterly swindling ordinary people. He's sold his body to you. He's put it over on one side. What's going on in your mind?
3. He just sees that the awl point is sharp; he doesn't see that the chisel edge is square. What is he saying? After all, he suffers defeat.
4. A hit! He should be hit—it won't do to let him go.
5. Grabbing the tiger's whiskers a second time. He's clutching the loot crying out that he's been wronged—why? East, west, south, north—the reflections and echoes are still present.

514

6. Again he's sold his body to you. A pitfall to trap tigers. What's going on in your mind?
7. He just sees that the awl point is sharp; he doesn't see that the chisel edge is square. Though he has waves that go against the current, yet he has no horns on his head. With a mouth full of blood, he spits out at people.
8. A hit! It won't do to let him go. He should be hit—why does T'ou Tzu stop before his staff is broken?

COMMENTARY

T'ou Tzu was plain and truthful; he had the eloquence which stood out from the crowd. Whenever a question was put to him, you saw his guts as soon as he opened his mouth. Without expending superfluous effort, he would immediately cut off the questioner's tongue. It could be said that, setting his plans in motion from within his headquarters tent, he decided victory beyond a thousand miles. This monk had taken his views of sound and form Buddhism and stuck them to his forehead: whenever he met someone, he would immediately ask about it. But T'ou Tzu, an adept, profoundly discerns oncoming winds.

Knowing that T'ou Tzu was truthful, this monk from the start was making a trap for him to go into—hence his subsequent remarks. Nevertheless it was T'ou Tzu who used the tiger trap to fish out the monk's subsequent words. This monk received T'ou Tzu's answer by saying, "Teacher, doesn't your asshole make farting sounds?" As it turned out, as soon as T'ou Tzu set his hook, the monk immediately climbed onto it. Anyone else would have been unable to handle this monk, but T'ou Tzu had the eye and followed up behind and hit him. Such "hound biting a boar" ability is only possible for an adept. Whether he turned to the left or to the right, T'ou Tzu followed him, turning smoothly. When this monk made a trap, wanting to grab the tiger's whiskers, he was far from knowing that T'ou Tzu was above his trap and would hit him. Too bad for this monk—he had a head but no tail. As soon as T'ou Tzu picked up his staff, the monk should have overturned his meditation seat. Then even if T'ou Tzu had used his full capacity, he still would have had to fall back three thousand miles.

The monk also asked, "Coarse words or subtle talk, all returns to the primary meaning—right or wrong?" Again T'ou
Tzu said, "Right." This is just like his previous answer; there is
no difference. When the monk said, "Can I call you an ass,
Teacher?" T'ou Tzu again hit him. Although this monk was
making himself a nest, nevertheless he was still exceptional. If
the old fellow up on the carved wood seat had been without an
eye on his forehead, it would have been impossible for him to
crush this monk. But T'ou Tzu did have a place to turn around.
When this monk made up a theory, he wanted to plunder T'ou
Tzu's shop; but in the end, as before, he couldn't cope with the
old fellow.

Haven't you seen Yen T'ou's saying? "In battle each one
occupies a pivotal position." T'ou Tzu let go very slowly and
gathered in very swiftly. At the time, if this monk had known
how to turn himself around and show some life, wouldn't he
have been able to act as a man with a mouth like a bowl of
blood? A patchrobed monk either doesn't act or (once he be-
gins) doesn't quit. Since this monk was unable to spring back,
his nostrils were pierced by T'ou Tzu. The verse says:

VERSE

T'ou Tzu! T'ou Tzu!
> Obviously there's no one on earth like this truthful old
> fellow. He spoils the sons and daughters of other people's
> families.

The wheel of his ability is unobstructed.
> What difficulty is there to handling him? There is a bit
> indeed.

He releases one and gets two—
> He snatches your eyes. Where will you see T'ou Tzu?

The same for that and the same for this.
> Act this way and you'll get a beating; don't act this way
> and you'll still get a beating. If you take this monk's place,
> I'll hit you.

How pitiful: innumerable people playing in the tide,
> The monasteries produce one or a half: they produced this
> fellow. The world's patchrobed monks act this way.

In the end fall into the tide and die.
  Too bad! What can they do? They can't get out of the trap.
  A sad person shouldn't talk to sad people.
If they suddenly came to life,
  My meditation seat shakes—he's startled me. I too fall
  back three thousand miles.
*The hundred rivers would reverse their flow with a rushing
    roaring noise.*
  Danger! It is useless to stop and think. I wouldn't dare
  open my mouth. Old man T'ou Tzu, too, must break his
  staff before he's all right.

COMMENTARY

"T'ou Tzu! T'ou Tzu!/The wheel of his ability is unobstructed." T'ou Tzu often said, "You always say that T'ou
Tzu is truthful, but if you suddenly went three steps down the
mountain and someone asked you, 'What is T'ou Tzu's truth-
fulness?' how would you respond?" The man of old Hsueh Tou
said, "Where the wheel of his ability turns the actor is still
deluded." The wheel of T'ou Tzu's ability turns so smoothly,
entirely without obstructions.
  Thus Hsueh Tou says, "He releases one and gets two."
Haven't you heard? A monk asked, "What is Buddha?" T'ou
Tzu said, "Buddha." Again he asked, "What is the Path?" T'ou
Tzu said, "The Path." Again he asked, "What is Ch'an?" T'ou
Tzu said, "Ch'an." He also asked, "How is it when the moon is
not yet full?" T'ou Tzu said, "Swallowing three or four." Again
he asked, "How is it after the moon is full?" T'ou Tzu said,
"Spitting out seven or eight." When T'ou Tzu received people
he always used this ability.
  When he answered this monk (in the main case) he just used
the one word "Right." This monk got hit both times. Hence
Hsueh Tou says, "The same for that and the same for this."
The first four lines have all at once completed Hsueh Tou's
praise of T'ou Tzu.
  At the end Hsueh Tou versifies the monk saying, "How
pitiful: innumerable people playing in the tide." This monk
dared to seize T'ou Tzu's banner and drums saying, "Teacher,
doesn't your asshole make farting sounds?" and "Can I call you

an ass, Teacher?" This then is where he played in the tide.
When this monk had exhausted his clever maneuvers, as before
he died amidst T'ou Tzu's words, so T'ou Tzu then hit him.
Thus this monk "In the end falls into the tide and dies."

Hsueh Tou releases this monk and says that if he suddenly
came to life and overturned the meditation seat, then even
T'ou Tzu would have to fall back three thousand miles, and
then "The hundred rivers would reverse their flow with a rushing roaring noise." Not only does my meditation seat shake,
but the mountains and rivers quake and heaven and earth are
abruptly blacked out. If each and every one of you were like
this, I'd be beating the drums of retreat. Where will all of you
go to secure your bodies and establish your lives?

Chao Chou's Newborn Baby

CASE

A monk asked Chao Chou, "Does a newborn baby also have the sixth consciousness?"[1] Chao Chou said, "(Like) tossing a ball on swift-flowing water."[2]

The monk also asked T'ou Tzu, "What is the meaning of 'Tossing a ball on swift-flowing water'?"[3] T'ou Tzu said, "Moment to moment, nonstop flow."[4]

NOTES

1. With a lightning flash intellect, what newborn baby is he talking about?
2. It's gone by. Even a swift hawk cannot overtake it. You still must check it out.
3. This too is adepts investigating together. Understand? It's gone by.
4. He's a fellow who creates complications.

COMMENTARY

In the school of the Teachings, this eighth consciousness is set up as the true basis. Mountains, rivers, and the great earth, sun, moon, and stars come into being because of it. It comes as the advance guard and leaves as the rearguard. The Ancients say that "The triple world is only mind—the myriad things are only consciousness." If one experiences the stage of Buddhahood, the eight consciousnesses are transformed into the four wisdoms.[a] In the school of the Teachings they call this "Changing names, not changing essence."

Sense-faculties, sense-objects, and consciousness of sensation are three. Originally we are unable to discriminate among the sense-objects before us. But the subtle inner faculties can produce consciousness, and consciousness can reveal discrimination of forms. This is the sixth consciousness—conceptual thinking. The seventh consciousness is Manas. It can go take hold of the imaginary things of the world and cause a person to be vexed and troubled so that he doesn't attain freedom and independence. As for the eighth consciousness, it's called the Alayavijnana and it's also called the Storehouse Consciousness. It contains all the seeds of good and evil.

This monk knew the ideas of the verbal teachings, so he used them to question Chao Chou by saying, "Does a newborn baby also have the sixth consciousness or not?" Although a newborn baby is equipped with the six consciousnesses, though his eyes can see and his ears can hear, he doesn't yet discriminate among the six sense-objects. At this time he knows nothing of good and evil, long and short, right and wrong, or gain and loss. A person who studies the Path must become again like an infant. Then praise and blame, success and fame, unfavorable circumstances and favorable environments—none of these can move him. "Though his eyes see form, he is the same as a blind man; though his ears hear sound, he is the same as a deaf man." He is like a fool, like an idiot—his mind is motionless as Mt. Sumeru. This is the place where patchrobed monks really and truly acquire power.

An Ancient said, "My patched garment covering my head, myriad concerns cease: at this time I don't understand anything at all." Only if you can be like this will you have a small share of attainment. Though an adept is like this, nevertheless he can't be fooled at all—as before, mountains are mountains and rivers are rivers. He is without artifice and without clinging thoughts. He is like the sun and moon moving through the sky without ever stopping and without saying, "I have so many names and forms." He is like the sky everywhere covering, like the earth everywhere supporting: since they have no mind, they bring up and nurture myriad beings without saying, "I have so many accomplishments." Since sky and earth are mindless, they last forever—what has mind has limits. A person who has attained the Path is like this too. In the midst of no activity, he carries out his activities, accepting all unfavorable and favorable circumstances with a compassionate heart.

When they got to this point the Ancients still upbraided themselves and said, "When you've completely perfectly comprehended, there's nothing to comprehend; in the dark, abstruse, hidden place, you still must be rebuked." They also said, "All things are thoroughly comprehended and all beings are clearly understood—when one who has Arrived senses this, he's startled in the darkness." Again it was said, "Without making a sound he goes beyond the ordinary and enters sagehood. The reclining dragon deeply fears the blue pool's clarity." If human beings can be like this always, how can a single name remain in the world? Though it's this way, they must go on to leap out of their nest before they attain.

Haven't you seen where it says in the (Hua Yen) sutra,[b] "A bodhisattva of the eighth stage, Immovability, turns the great Dharma Wheel in an atom of dust, using the wisdom of non-activity. At all times, whether walking, standing, sitting, or lying down, he doesn't cling to gain and loss, but lets himself move and flow into the sea of All-Knowledge." When patch-robed monks get here they still must not become attached: they follow the occasion freely. When they have tea, they drink tea; when they have food, they eat food. Neither the words "concentration" nor "not concentration" can be applied to this transcendental matter.

Master Shan Tao of the Stone Grotto taught his congregation saying, "Haven't you seen a little one when it's just emerged from the womb? Has a baby ever said, 'I know how to read the scriptures'? At that time it does not know the meaning of having the Buddha nature or not having the Buddha nature. As he grows up he learns all sorts of knowledge; then he comes forth saying 'I am able' and 'I understand,' without knowing that this is troubling over illusory dusts. Among the sixteen contemplation practices, the baby's practice is the best. When he's babbling he symbolizes the person studying the Path, with his detachment from the discriminating mind that grasps and rejects. That's why I'm praising infants. I can make a comparison by taking the case of a baby, but if I say that the baby is the Path, people of these times would misunderstand."

Nan Ch'uan said, "After eighteen, I was able to make a living." Chao Chou said, "After eighteen, I was able to break up the family and scatter the household." He also said, "I was in the South for twenty years: only the two mealtimes of gruel and rice were points of mixed application of mind."

Ts'ao Shan asked a monk, "'In his concentration the bodhisattva smells the fragrant elephant crossing the river very

THE BLUE CLIFF RECORD

clearly.' What scripture does this come from?" The monk said, "From the *Nirvana* scripture." Shan said, "Does he smell it before or after his concentration?" The monk said "You've flowed, Teacher." Shan said, "Receive it on the river bank."

Again: the *Surangama* scripture says, "The fullness (of the six consciousnesses) enters to merge in the fullness (of the Storehouse Consciousness), going into the realm of consciousness."

Again: the *Lankavatara* scripture says, "Birth of signs— being obstructed by grasping. Birth of conception—false thinking. Birth of flow—pursuing falsehood, revolving and flowing. You must get out of the third aspect, 'birth of flow'; only then will you be joyfully alive and independent."*c*

Thus Kuei Shan asked Yang Shan, "How is it with you Disciple Chi?" Yang Shan said, "Are you asking about his perceptive understanding or his active understanding? If you ask about his active understanding, I don't know. If you ask about his perceptive understanding, it's like a pitcher of water being poured into a pitcher of water." If you can be like this you can be the teacher of a region.

When Chao Chou said, "Tossing a ball on swift-flowing water," he was already turning smoothly. When you toss it onto swift-flowing water, in a blink of an eye it's gone. As the *Surangama* scripture says, "Looked upon from afar, swift-flowing water is tranquil and still." An Ancient said, "In a fast-flowing river the currents of water never stop and they are unaware of each other—all things are like this too." The meaning of Chao Chou's answer is completely similar to these (quotations).

The monk also asked T'ou Tzu, "What is the meaning of 'Tossing a ball on swift-flowing water'?" T'ou Tzu said, "Moment to moment, nonstop flow," spontaneously matching the monk's question perfectly. The practice of these Ancients, Chao Chou and T'ou Tzu, was so thoroughgoing that they answered as one. They no longer make use of calculations—as soon as you question them they already know where you come down.

Although a baby's sixth consciousness is inactive, nevertheless from moment to moment it doesn't stop, but flows on like a hidden river. Of T'ou Tzu's answering this way we can say that he profoundly discerns oncoming winds.

Hsueh Tou's verse says:

VERSE

Sixth consciousness inactive—he puts forth a question.
Though he has eyes, he is like a blind man; though he has
ears, he is like a deaf man. The bright mirror is in its
stand; the bright pearl is in the palm of his hand. In one
line Hsueh Tou has said it all.

The adepts have both discerned where he's coming from—
What's the need? Still, one must distinguish initiated
from naive. Just experience it, then you'll know.

On the boundless swift-flowing water, tossing a ball:
Consistent from beginning to end. It's gone. What is he
saying?

Where it comes down, it doesn't stay—who can watch it?
Watch it and you'll go blind. It's gone. "Receive it on the
river bank."

COMMENTARY

"Sixth consciousness inactive—he puts forth a question."
When the Ancients studied the Path they brought themselves
to this point: this is called "achievement of non-activity."
They were the same as a newborn baby: though possessed of
eyes, ears, nose, tongue, body, and mind, they didn't discriminate among the six sense-objects. In sum, they were non-
active. When you get to this realm, then you can overcome
dragons and subdue tigers, die sitting or die standing up. Right
now people should just take the myriad phenomena before
their eyes and put them to rest at once. What need is there to
get above the eighth stage (of a bodhisattva) before you can be
like this? Although there's no activity, as of old mountains are
mountains and rivers are rivers.

In a previous verse (about Chao Chou and T'ou Tzu, in Case
41) Hsueh Tou said, "In living there's an eye—still, it's the
same as death/Why use anti-serum to test an adept?" Since
Chao Chou and T'ou Tzu were adepts he says, "The adepts

have both discerned where he's coming from—/On the boundless swift-flowing water, tossing a ball." T'ou Tzu said, "Moment to moment, nonstop flow." Do all of you people know
what this really means? At the end Hsueh Tou has people set
eyes on it for themselves and watch. Hence he says, "Where it
comes down, it doesn't stay—who can watch it?" This is
Hsueh Tou's living line. But say, what does it really mean?

TRANSLATORS' NOTES

a. The eight consciousnesses are transformed into four knowledges
as follows: The first five consciousnesses (associated with seeing,
hearing, tasting, smelling, and touching) are transmuted into the
Knowledge of Accomplishment. The sixth consciousness becomes the Wondrous Observing Knowledge, the seventh becomes
the Knowledge of Equality, and the eighth becomes the Great
Perfect Mirror Knowledge.

b. The ten stages of a bodhisattva's career, as described in the Hua
Yen (Avatamsaka) scripture, are called: 1) Joy; 2) Freedom from
Defilement; 3) Emanating Light; 4) Radiant Wisdom; 5) Impossi-
ble to Surpass; 6) (True Thusness) Becoming Manifest; 7) Far-
reaching; 8) Immovability; 9) Good Wisdom; 10) Clouds of
Dharma.

c. Kuei Shan said to Yang Shan, "I consider the Mirror Knowledge to
be the source of the school. It produces three kinds of birth: birth
of conception, birth of signs, birth of flowings. The Surangama
scripture says, 'Concepts and signs constitute the dusts; conscious feelings constitute defilement. Detach from both and your
Dharma Eye will be clear and pure at all times: how could you fail
then to realize unexcelled correct awakening?' The birth of conception is fragmentation and confusion of the mind which thinks;
the birth of signs is the manifestation of the object thought of.
Together with the subtle flowings, they constitute the dusts and
defilements. If you can clear them completely, only then will you
be free." (Jen T'ien Yen Mu, 3)

Yao Shan's Shooting the Elk of Elks

POINTER

He captures the banner and seizes the drums—the thousand sages cannot search him out. He cuts off confusing obscurities—ten thousand devices cannot get to him. This is not the wondrous functioning of spiritual powers, nor is it the suchness of the basic essence. But tell me, what does he rely on to attain such marvels?

CASE

A monk asked Yao Shan, "On a level field, in the shallow grass, the elk and deer form a herd: how can one shoot the elk of elks?"[1] Shan said, "Look—an arrow!"[2] The monk let himself fall down.[3] Shan said, "Attendant, drag this dead fellow out."[4] The monk then ran out.[5] Shan said, "This fellow playing with a mud ball—what end will there be to it?"[6]

Hsueh Tou commented saying, "Though he lived for three steps, after five steps he had to die."[7]

NOTES

1. He enters enemy headquarters with his helmet off. He raises his head wearing horns. He pulls an arrow out of the back of his head.[a]
2. He goes right up and takes him. If you're not running downhill fast, it's hard to meet him. A hit!
3. Obviously this monk is unusual, but once dead he doesn't come to life again. He's a fellow giving play to his spirit.
4. He acts according to the imperative. He doesn't bother to test the monk again. The first arrow was still light; the second arrow was deep.

5. Inside the coffin, he opens up his eyes—within death he finds life. He still has some breath left.
6. Too bad Yao Shan let him go. He acts according to the imperative, but he's adding frost on top of snow.
7. One hand lifts up, one hand presses down. Even if he ran a hundred steps he would still have to lose his body and his life.

COMMENTARY

In the Ts'ao Tung tradition this case is called "a question that uses things." It's also called "a question testing the host," used in order to illustrate his present state of mind.

Ordinarily deer and elk are easy to shoot. Only the elk of elks, that is, the king among deer, is very difficult to shoot. This (king) elk always sharpens his horns on the rocks of the cliffs (where it lives,) so that they become sharp as sword blades. He defends the herd of deer with his own body so that even tigers cannot come near.

Likewise, this monk seems intelligent and alert as he draws on this to question Yao Shan to reveal what he would do first. Shan said, "Look—an arrow!" An expert Teaching Master, he is undeniably marvellous, like sparks struck from stone, like a flash of lightning.

Haven't you heard (about what happened) when San P'ing first called on Shih Kung? As soon as Kung saw him coming, he immediately went through the motion of bending a bow and said, "Look—an arrow!" San P'ing opened his breast (to the "arrow") and said, "This is the arrow that kills the man—what is the arrow that brings the man life?" Kung plucked the bowstring three times, whereupon San P'ing bowed in homage. Kung said, "After thirty years with a single bow and two arrows, today I've finally managed to shoot half a sage." Then he broke his bow and arrows.

Later San P'ing took this up with Ta Tien. Tien said, "Since it is the arrow that brings people life, why draw it on a bowstring?" an P'ing was speechless. Tien said, "Thirty years hence it will still be hard to find someone to raise these words."

Fa Teng had a verse saying:

In the old days we had Master Shih Kung—
Setting his bow and arrows, he sat.
He went on like this for thirty years—
Not a single one understood (until)
San P'ing came and hit the target,
And father and son reached harmony.
Thinking back carefully, (I see that)
From the beginning, they were shooting the mound
*   (instead of the target on it.)*

Shih Kung's strategy was the same as Yao Shan's. San P'ing had an eye on his forehead, so he hit the target immediately given a single phrase. It was just like Yao Shan saying, "Look—an arrow!" and this monk then letting himself fall down, playing the elk. This monk seemed to be an adept too, but it's just that he had a head but no tail. Once he had set his trap, he wanted to make Yao Shan fall in. But what could he do? Yao Shan was an adept and kept on pressing relentlessly. When Shan said, "Attendant, drag this dead fellow out," it was as if he was extending his battle lines forward. This monk then ran out: he may have been right, but nonetheless he wasn't free and clean, his hands and feet were stuck. That's why Yao Shan said, "This fellow playing with a mud ball—what end will there be to it?" If Yao Shan hadn't had the final word at that time, he would have been criticized by others down through the ages.

Shan said, "Look—an arrow!" whereupon this monk fell down. Tell me, was this understanding or not? If you say it was understanding, why then did Yao Shan speak of him this way, as a fellow playing with a mud ball? This was extremely evil, just like (the following):

A monk asked Te Shan, "How is it when a student holding a sharp sword tries to take the Master's head?" Te Shan extended his neck forward toward him and shouted. The monk said, "The Master's head has fallen." Te Shan lowered his head and returned to his abbot's quarters. Again: Yen T'ou asked a monk, "Where have you come from?" The monk said, "From the Western Capital." Yen T'ou said, "After Huang Ch'ao passed by, did you take his sword?" The monk said, "I did." Yen T'ou extended his neck forward toward him and shouted. The monk said, "The Master's head has fallen." Yen T'ou laughed loudly. Cases of this kind are all traps to fell tigers, just like the present main case. Fortunately Yao Shan wasn't taken in by this monk—since he saw through him, he just kept on pressing.

Hsueh Tou says, "Although this monk lived for three steps, after five steps he had to die." Although this monk knew very well how to look at the arrow, he immediately let himself fall down—when Yao Shan said, "Attendant, drag this dead fellow out," he immediately ran out. Hsueh Tou says, "I'm afraid he won't live beyond three steps." If the monk had leaped beyond five steps at that time, no one in the world would have been able to handle him.

In a meeting of adepts, from beginning to end there must be an uninterrupted interchange of guest and host; only then is there a share of freedom and independence. Since at that time the monk wasn't able to continue from beginning to end, consequently he meets with Hsueh Tou's censure. But at the end Hsueh Tou himself uses his words for his verse saying:

VERSE

The elk of elks—
    Set your eyes high and look! He raises his head wearing horns.
You should take a look.
    What sort of thing is it? He's running in the secondary level. If you want to shoot, then shoot, but why look?
(Yao Shan) releases one arrow—
    On target. You must realize that Yao Shan is an expert.
(The monk) runs three steps.
    He's leaping with life, but only for three steps. He's been dead a long time.
If he had lived for five steps,
    What for? He leaps a hundred steps. How is it when unexpectedly finding life in the midst of death?
He would have formed a herd and chased the tiger.
    The two reflect each other. You should fall back three thousand miles. The world's patchrobed monks let the tiger get away.

The correct eye has always been given to a hunter.
What can you do? Yao Shan doesn't consent to acknowl-
edge these words. It's so for Yao Shan—what about Hsueh
Tou? It doesn't concern Yao Shan, it doesn't concern
Hsueh Tou, it doesn't concern me, and it doesn't concern
you.

In a loud voice Hsueh Tou said, "Look—an arrow!"
One punishment for all their crimes. You must fall back
three thousand miles from them before you're all right. I
hit, saying, "He's already blocked off your throats."

COMMENTARY

"The elk of elks—you should take a look." Patchrobed monks
must have the eye of the elk of elks and the horns of the elk of
elks, they must have devices and strategy. Even if it's a fierce
tiger with wings or a great cat with horns, the elk of elks can
still preserve his body and keep harm at a distance. At that
time when this monk let himself fall, he was saying of himself,
"I am the elk of elks."

"Yao Shan releases one arrow—the monk runs three steps."
When Yao Shan said, "Look—an arrow!" the monk then fell
down. When Yao Shan said, "Attendant, drag this dead fellow
out," the monk then ran out. He did very well, but nevertheless he was only able to run three steps.

"If he had lived for five steps,/He would have formed a herd
and chased the tiger." Hsueh Tou said, "I'm afraid that after
five steps he had to die. If he had been able to leap beyond five
steps at that time, then he would have been able to gather his
herd and gone to chase the tiger." The horns of the elk of elks
are sharp as spears—when a tiger sees him, even he becomes
afraid and flees. This elk is the king among the deer: he always
leads the herd in driving the tiger to another mountain.

Finally Hsueh Tou praises Yao Shan for having a way to
assert himself in that situation. "The correct eye had always
been given to a hunter." Yao Shan is like a hunter who knows
how to shoot and this monk is like (his quarry) the elk. Then,
having gone up to the hall and related this story, Hsueh Tou
wrapped it up into a single bundle, speaking a single line in a
loud voice: "Look—an arrow!" At once those who had been
sitting and standing (listening to him) were unable to stir.

TRANSLATORS' NOTES

a.   "He pulls an arrow out of the back of his head": the arrow pierces his head from the front; he pulls it all the way through and out the back.

Ta Lung's Hard and Fast Body of Reality

POINTER

Only those with eyes can know the fishing line. Only adepts can handle devices outside of patterns. But say, what is the fishing line? What are devices beyond patterns? To test I'm citing this old case: look!

CASE

A monk asked Ta Lung, "The physical body rots away: what is the hard and fast body of reality?"[1]

Lung said, "The mountain flowers bloom like brocade, the valley streams are brimming blue as indigo."[2]

NOTES

1. His statement makes them into two. Still, it's all right to separate them.
2. A flute with no holes hitting against a felt-pounding board. The whole cannot be broken apart. When someone comes from one end of the province, I go to the other end.

COMMENTARY

If you go to the words to search for this thing, it's like trying to hit the moon by waving a stick—you won't make any connection. An Ancient clearly stated, "If you want to attain Intimacy, don't ask with questions. Why? Because the question is in the answer and the answer is in the question."

This monk picked up a load of crudeness and exchanged it for a load of confusion: in posing this question, his defeat was not slight. How could anyone other than Ta Lung manage to cover heaven and cover earth? The monk asking this way and Ta Lung answering this way is a single whole. Ta Lung didn't move a hair's breadth: it was like seeing a rabbit and releasing a falcon, like seeing a hole and putting in a plug. Is this time and season in the twelve-part canon of the Triple Vehicle? Undeniably his answer was extraordinary, it's just that his words have no flavor and he blocks up people's mouths. Thus it is said, "When white clouds lie across the valley mouth, many birds returning by night can't find their nests."

Some say that this was just answering glibly. Those who understand in this fashion are nothing but exterminators of the Buddha's race. They are far from knowing that with one device and one objective, the Ancients broke fetters and smashed chains, that every word and phrase were pure gold and raw gems.

If one has the eye and brain of a patchrobed monk, sometimes he holds fast and sometimes he lets go. Shining and functioning at the same time, with both persons and objects taken away, both sides let go and both sides gather in. Facing the situation, he changes accordingly. Without the great function and great capacity, how would he be able to enclose heaven and earth like this? Much as a bright mirror on its stand: when a foreigner comes, a foreigner appears, and when a native comes, a native appears.

This case is the same as the story (case 39) of the Flower Hedge, though the meaning is not the same. Here the monk's question was ignorant, so Ta Lung's answer was exactly appropriate. Haven't you heard (this story, case 27)? A monk asked Yun Men, "How is it when the tree withers and the leaves fall?" Men said, "The body exposed in the golden wind." This is called "arrowpoints meeting." Here the monk asked Ta Lung, "The physical body rots away: what is the hard and fast body of reality?" Ta Lung said, "The mountain flowers bloom like brocade, the valley streams are brimming blue as indigo." This is just like "you go west to Ch'in, I go east to Lu": since he acts this way, I don't act this way. Matching Ta Lung's answer with Yun Men's, they're opposites. It's easy to see Yun Men acting thus, but it's hard to see Ta Lung acting otherwise. Nevertheless, Ta Lung's tongue is very subtle.

VERSE

Asking without knowing.
> East and west not distinguished. Playing with the thing without knowing its name. He buys the hat to fit the head.

Answering, still not understanding.
> South and north not differentiated. He switched the monk's skull around. South of the river, north of the river.

The moon is cold, the wind is high—
> What is it like? Today is precisely this time and season. The world's people have eyes but have never seen, have ears but have never heard.

On the ancient cliff, frigid juniper.
> Even better when it's not raining. A flute with no holes hitting against a felt-pounding board.

How delightful: on the road he met a man who had attained the Path,
> You too must get here personally before you're all right. Give me back my staff. They come like this, forming a crowd.

And didn't use speech or silence to reply.
> Where will you see Ta Lung? What would you use to answer him properly?

His hand grasps the white jade whip.
> It should be broken to pieces.

And smashes the black dragon's pearl.[a]
> It remains for future people to look at. Too bad!

If he hadn't smashed it,
> Letting his move go. Again you go on like this.

He would have increased its flaws.
> What is he doing, playing with a mud ball? He seems more and more decrepit. His crimes fill the sky.

The nation has a code of laws—
> Those who know the law fear it. "In the morning three thousand blows, at night eight hundred blows."

Three thousand articles of offenses.
> He's only told the half of it. There are eighty-four thousand. Countless eons of uninterrupted hell wouldn't make up for half of it.

COMMENTARY

Hsueh Tou versifies here with much skill. Before when he was versifying Yun Men's words ("body exposed in the golden wind") he said, "Since the question has the source/The answer too is in the same place." Since it's not so with this case, Hsueh Tou instead says, "Asking without knowing/ Answering, still not understanding." Ta Lung's answer was a glimpse from the side that was simply amazing. His answer was so clear that whoever questioned him this way had already incurred defeat even before he asked. With his answer he was able to bend down to the monk and match him perfectly: adapting to his capacity he rightly said, "The mountain flowers bloom like brocade, the valley streams are brimming blue as indigo." How will all of you understand Ta Lung's meaning right now? As a glimpse from the side, his answer was truly extraordinary.

Thus Hsueh Tou comes out with his verse to make people realize that the moon is cold, the wind is high and still beats against the frigid juniper on the ancient cliff. But say, how will you understand Hsueh Tou's meaning? Thus I just said that it's a flute with no holes hitting against a felt-pounding board.

The verse is completed with just these first four lines, but Hsueh Tou was still fearful that people would make up rationalizations, so he said, "How delightful: on the road he met a man who had attained the Path,/And didn't use speech or silence to reply." This matter, then, is not seeing, hearing, discernment, or knowledge; nor is it the discriminations of calculating thought. Therefore it was said:

> *Direct and truthful, without bringing anything else along,*

Moving on alone—what is there to depend on?
On the road, if you meet anyone who has attained
  the Path,
Don't use speech or silence to reply.

This is a verse of Hsiang Yen's that Hsueh Tou has drawn on. Haven't you heard? A monk asked Chao Chou, "Without using speech or silence to answer, I wonder with what should one answer?" Chou said, "Show your lacquer vessel." These (sayings of Hsiang Yen and Chao Chou) are the same as Ta Lung's statement (in the main case): they don't fall within the scope of your feelings or conceptual thoughts.

What is this like? "His hand grasps the white jade whip/And smashes the black dragon's pearl." Thus the command of the patriarchs must be carried out, cutting off everything in the ten directions. This is the matter on the sword's edge, for which one must have this kind of strategy. Otherwise you turn your back on all the sages since antiquity. When you get here you must be without the slightest concern, then naturally you'll have the advantage. This, then, is how a transcendent man comports himself. "If he hadn't smashed it," necessarily "He would have increased its flaws," and thus he would have seemed broken down and decrepit.

But in the end, how can you be right? "The nation has a code of laws—/Three thousand articles of offenses." There are three thousand subdivisions of the five punishments, and none is greater than (the punishment) for not being respectful. This monk offended against all three thousand articles at once. How so? Because he didn't deal with people on the basis of his own thing. As for Ta Lung, he of course was not this way.

TRANSLATORS' NOTES

a. This precious jewel of legend is to be found in the ocean depths, right under the jaws of the black dragon.

Yun Men's Ancient Buddhas and the Pillar

CASE

Yun Men, teaching the community, said, "The ancient Buddhas and the pillar merge—what level of mental activity is this?"[1] He himself said on their behalf,[2] "On South Mountain clouds gather,[3] on North Mountain rain falls."[4]

NOTES

1. Three thousand miles away. There's no connection. Cracked open.
2. When someone in the eastern house dies, someone from the western house assists in the mourning. The single compounded form cannot be grasped.
3. Throughout heaven and earth, they can't be seen. A knife cannot cut through.
4. Not a drop falls. Half south of the river, half north of the river.

COMMENTARY

Great Master Yun Men produced more than eighty men of knowledge. Seventeen years after he passed on, when they opened his tomb and beheld him, (his body was not decomposed, but) upright and sound as formerly. The field of his vision had been bright and clear, his mentality and perspective swift. All his instructions, alternative remarks, and words spoken on behalf of others were direct, solitary, and steep. This present case is like sparks struck from stone, like flashing lightning; in fact, it's "a spirit appearing and a demon disappearing."[a] Librarian Ch'ing said, "Is there such talk in the whole great treasury of the Teachings?"

536

People these days make their living on emotional interpretations and say "Buddha is the guide for the three realms, the compassionate father of the four orders of living beings. Why then do the ancient Buddhas merge with the pillar?" If you understand this way, you'll never be able to find it. Some call (Yun Men's saying) "calling out from within nothingness." They are far from knowing that the talk of the teaching masters of our school cuts off conceptual consciousness, cuts off emotional evaluation, cuts off birth and death, and cuts off the defilement of doctrine, enters the correct state[b] without retaining anything at all. As soon as you rationalize and calculate, you tie your hands and feet.

But tell me, what was old Yun Men's meaning? Just make mind and objects a single thusness; then good and bad, right and wrong, won't be able to shake you. Then it will be all right whether you say "there is" or "there isn't"; then it will be all right whether you have mental activity or you don't. When you get here, each and every clap of the hands is the true imperative. My late teacher Wu Tsu said, "Yun Men, supposedly so great, really didn't have much guts." If it were me, I just would have told him, "The eighth level of mental activity."

He said, "The ancient Buddhas and the pillar merge—what level of mental activity is this?" In that moment he wrapped it all up in front of you. When a monk asked him what this meant, Yun Men said, "one belt worth thirty cents." He has the eye to judge heaven and earth.

Since no one understood, afterwards he himself spoke on their behalf: "On South Mountain clouds gather, on North Mountain rain falls." Thus he opened up a route of entry for future students. That's why Hsueh Tou picks out the place where he settles heaven and earth to make people see. But as soon as you blunder into calculation, you stumble past and miss it, though it's right in front of you. You simply must go to the source of Yun Men's fundamental meaning to clearly understand his lofty mind. Thus the verse says,

VERSE

South Mountain clouds,
  Throughout heaven and earth, they can't be seen. A knife cannot cut in.

North Mountain rain—
> Not a drop falls. Half south of the river, half north of the river.

The Twenty-Eight and Six see it before them.
> Wherever I look, I can't see. Hsueh Tou is dragging in other people. The lantern is hanging from the pillar.

In Korea they've gone up into the hall,
> Surging up in the east, sinking down in the west. The east guild doesn't see the profits of the west guild. Where does he get this news?

In China they haven't yet beaten the drum.
> Fifteen minutes late. Give me back the story. At first he doesn't get there, afterwards he goes too far.

In suffering, happiness—
> Who would you have know this?

In happiness, suffering—
> A double case. Who would you have bring this up? Suffering is suffering, happiness is happiness. Where are there two heads, three faces?

Who says gold is like shit?
> Those with eyes will discern this. Try to brush it off and look. Uh-oh! What a pity! But say, is it the ancient Buddhas or the pillar?

COMMENTARY

"South Mountain clouds, / North Mountain rain." Hsueh Tou buys the hat to fit the head, watches the wind to set his sails. On the edge of a sword, he puts down footnotes for you. As for "The Twenty-eight (Indian Ch'an Patriarchs) and Six (Chinese Ch'an Patriarchs) see it before them," don't misunderstand! This simply versifies "The ancient Buddhas and the pillar merge—what level of mental activity is this?"

Afterwards, Hsueh Tou opens up a road and creates complications to make you see Yun Men's meaning. "In Korea they've gone up into the hall, / In China they haven't yet beaten the drum." Hsueh Tou goes where the thunder rolls and comets fly and says, "In suffering, happiness— / In happiness, suffering."

Hsueh Tou seems to have piled up gems and jewels and put them here.

Finally there's this little line, "Who says gold is like shit?" This line is from Ch'an Yueh's poem "Travelling the Road is Hard," which Hsueh Tou draws on here to use. Ch'an Yueh wrote,

> *People cannot fathom the ocean's depth or the*
> *mountains' height—*
> *Past and present, more and more green and blue.*
> *Don't associate with the shallow and superficial—*
> *Where the ground is low it can only produce bram-*
> *bles.*
> *Who says gold is like shit!*
> *No more news of Chang Er and Ch'en Yu.*[c]
> *Travelling the road is hard;*
> *The hardships of travel, see for yourself!*

And isn't the territory broad and the people few? You cloud-dwelling saints!

TRANSLATORS' NOTES

a. This term is used to describe the maneuvers of a skilled battle commander, who can direct his forces in unexpected movements that are baffling and unpredictable to the enemy.

b. In early Buddhism, the "correct state" means *nirvana*, the extinction of egoism and suffering. In the Ts'ao-Tung Ch'an tradition, the "correct state" was used to refer to emptiness as opposed (propositionally in dialectic and subjectively in meditation) to the "biased state," or the realm of myriad forms. The patriarchs of the Ts'ao-Tung school used a five step dialectic to show that the correct and biased simultaneously contain each other, and that each (defined as separate under the aforementioned conditions) has both a correct and biased, or absolute and relative, aspect. Of the correct, or absolute, Ts'ao Shan said, "This correct state does not come from illumination; it is so whether or not the Buddhas appear in the world. Thus all the thousand sages, the myriad sages, return to the correct state to attain realization" (from *Wu I Hsien Chueh,* "Revealing the Secret of the Five Ranks").

c. Chang Er and Ch'en Yu are the proverbial close friends who fell
    out and turned against each other. During the period of the fall of
    the Ch'in dynasty (end of the third century B.C.) Ch'en Yu's
    father had occupied territory with his army and begun to revive
    an independent state of Chao. (China had been unified for the first
    time under the Ch'in dynasty, which had conquered the six other
    major states, one of which was Chao.) Chang Er was an important
    minister in Chao under the Ch'ens. Later the friendship between
    Chang Er and Ch'en Yu turned to hatred, and Chang Er cooper-
    ated with the forces of one of the generals of the founder of the
    Han dynasty (which eventually succeeded Ch'in), which de-
    stroyed independent Chao and killed Ch'en Yu.

EIGHTY-FOURTH CASE

Vimalakirti's Gate of Nonduality

POINTER

Though you say "It is," there is nothing which "is" can affirm.
Though you say "It is not," there is nothing that "is not" can
negate. When "is" and "is not" are left behind, and gain and
loss are forgotten, then you are clean and naked, free and at
ease.

But tell me, what is in front of you and in back of you? If
there is a patchrobed monk who comes forward and says, "In
front is the Buddha shrine and the main gate, behind is the
abbot's sleeping room and private quarters," tell me, does this
man have eyes or not? If you can judge this man, I'll allow that
you have personally seen the Ancients.

CASE

Vimalakirti asked Manjusri,[1] "What is a bodhisattva's entry
into the Dharma gate of nonduality?"[2]
Manjusri said, "According to what I think,[3] in all things,[4] no
words, no speech,[5] no demonstration and no recognition,[6] to
leave behind all questions and answers;[7] this is entering the
Dharma gate of nonduality."[8]
Then Manjusri asked Vimalakirti, "We have each already
spoken. Now you should tell us, good man, what is a
bodhisattva's entry into the Dharma gate of nonduality?"[9]
Hsueh Tou said, "What did Vimalakirti say?"[10] He also said,
"Completely exposed."[11]

NOTES

1. This fellow is making quite a fuss. He should shut his mouth.
2. He knows, yet he deliberately transgresses.
3. What will he say? It simply can't be explained. He's wearing

stocks, carrying evidence of his crime, hauling himself into the magistrate's office.

4. What is he calling "all things"?
5. What is he saying?
6. He can fool others . . .
7. What is he saying?
8. What's the use of entering? What's the use of so many complications?
9. Not even the Buddhas of the past, present, and future, let alone the Golden Grain Tathagata (Vimalakirti), can open their mouths about this one support. Manjusri has turned the spear around and stabbed one man to death. The arrow hits Vimalakirti just as he was shooting at the others.
10. Bah! Hsueh Tou gathers ten thousand arrows to his breast and speaks the truth in Vimalakirti's place.
11. Not only that time, but now too, it is so. Hsueh Tou is drawing his bow after the thief has gone. Although he uses all his strength to help the congregation, what can he do—calamity comes forth from his own door. But tell me, can Hsueh Tou see where this comes down? Since he hasn't seen it even in a dream, how can he say "completely exposed"? Danger! Even the golden-haired lion is unable to search it out.

COMMENTARY

Vimalakirti had the various great bodhisattvas each speak on the Dharma gate of nonduality. At the time, the thirty-two bodhisattvas all took dualistic views of doing and nondoing, of the two truths, real and conventional, and merged them into a monistic view which they considered to be the Dharma gate of nonduality.

Finally he asked Manjusri. Manjusri said, "According to what I think, in all things, no words and no speech, no demonstration and no recognition, to leave behind all questions and answers; this is entering the Dharma gate of nonduality." Since the other thirty-two had used words to dispense with words, Manjusri used no-words to dispense with words. At once he swept everything away, not wanting anything, and considered this to be the Dharma gate of nonduality. He certainly didn't realize that this was the sacred tortoise dragging its tail, that in wiping away the tracks he was making traces. It's just like a broom sweeping away dust; though the dust is removed, the tracks of the broom still remain.

Since in the end, as before, some traces were left, Manjusri then asked Vimalakirti, "We have each already spoken. Now you tell us, good man, what is a bodhisattva's entry into the Dharma gate of nonduality?" Vimalakirti was silent. If you're alive, you'll never go sink into the dead water. If you make up such (dead) views, you're like a mad dog chasing a clod of earth.[a]

Hsueh Tou didn't say that Vimalakirti kept silent, nor did he say that he sat silently on his seat. Hsueh Tou just went to the critical point and said, "What did Vimalakirti say?" Just when Hsueh Tou spoke this way, did he see Vimalakirti? He hadn't seen him even in a dream.

Vimalakirti was an ancient Buddha of the past, who also had a family and household. He helped the Buddha Shakyamuni teach and transform. He had inconceivable intelligence, inconceivable perspective, inconceivable supernatural powers and the wondrous use of them. Inside his own room he accommodated thirty-two thousand jeweled lion thrones and a great multitude of eighty thousand, without it being too spacious or too crowded. But tell me, what principle is this? Can it be called the wondrous function of supernatural powers? Don't misunderstand; if it is the Dharma gate of nonduality, only by attaining together and witnessing together can there be common mutual realization and knowledge.

Only Manjusri was able to give a reply. Even so, was he able to avoid Hsueh Tou's censure? Hsueh Tou, talking as he did, also had to meet with these two men (Vimalakirti and Manjusri). Hsueh Tou said, "What did Vimalakirti say?" and "Completely exposed." You tell me, where was the exposure? This little bit has nothing to do with gain or loss, nor does it fall into right and wrong. It's like being up on a ten thousand fathom cliff; if you can give up your life and leap off, you may see Vimalakirti in person. If you cannot give it up, you're like a ram caught in a fence. Hsueh Tou was a man who had abandoned his life, so he produces it in verse, saying,

VERSE

Bah! to old Vimalakirti—
Why revile him? In the morning, three thousand blows, in the evening, eight hundred blows. Reviling him doesn't accomplish anything. He deserves thirty blows.

Out of compassion for living beings, he suffers an empty affliction,
Why have compassion for them? They themselves have the Diamond King's jewel sword. For this idle affair Vimalakirti increased their ignorance. He took the trouble but accomplished nothing.

Lying ill in Vaisali,
On whose account does he do this? It involves everyone.

His whole body withered and emaciated.[b]
Leaving aside his illness for a moment, why was his mouth bent into a frown? He can't eat food or draw a breath.

Manjusri, the teacher of seven Buddhas, comes
When a guest comes, one must attend to him. When a thief comes, one must beat him. Manjusri brings along a crowd. It takes an adept for this.

To the single room that's been swept repeatedly;
It still exists. From the beginning Vimalakirti has been making his living inside a ghost cave.

He asks about the gate of nonduality.
If there were anything that could be said, it would have been said by him. I hit, saying, "You too have searched without finding it."

Then Vimalakirti leans and falls.
Heavens! Heavens! What are you saying?

He doesn't lean and fall—
He finds life in the midst of death; there's still some breath in him.

The golden-haired lion has no place to look.
Bah! Do you see?

COMMENTARY

Hsueh Tou says "Bah! to old Vimalakirti!" Why does he start off at the very beginning reviling him? Right at the start Hsueh Tou takes the Diamond King's jewel sword and cuts him right off. Vimalakirti must be given three thousand blows in the morning and eight hundred blows in the evening.

In Sanskrit, Vimalakirti means "undefiled repute" or "pure name." He was also known as the Golden Grain Tathagata. Haven't you heard how a monk asked Master Chien of Yun Chu, "If he was the Golden Grain Tathagata, why then did he listen to the Dharma in the congregation of the Tathagata Shakyamuni?" Chien said, "He didn't contend over self and others. Someone who is greatly liberated has nothing to do with 'becoming Buddha' or 'not becoming Buddha.' If you say that he practices cultivation and strives to attain the Path of Buddhahood, this has even less to do with it." As the Perfect Enlightenment Scripture says, "If you use your routine mind to produce routine views, you will never be able to enter the Tathagata's great ocean of peaceful extinction."

Yung Chia said, "Whether he's right or wrong, people cannot know. Whether he goes against or goes along, the gods cannot fathom. If he goes along, then he turns toward the stage of the fruition of Buddhahood; if he goes against, then he enters the realms of sentient beings." Meditation Master Shou said, "Even if you can perfect yourself and get to this realm, you still can't follow your inclinations. Only when you have experienced the holy state without leaks can you go along or go against." Thus Hsueh Tou said, "Out of compassion for living beings, he suffers empty affliction." In the scripture Vimalakirti says, "Since sentient beings have illnesses, I also will have an illness." Hsueh Tou says, "Lying ill in Vaisali," because Vimalakirti manifested his illness in the city of Vaisali.

"His whole body withered and emaciated." Vimalakirti used his physical illness to preach the Dharma widely. He said, "This body has no permanence, no strength, no power or solidity; it's a thing that quickly decays, it can't be trusted. It produces suffering and trouble, a mass of diseases. It is something made of the heaps, elements, and sense media compounded together."

"The teacher of seven Buddhas comes." Manjusri was the teacher of seven Buddhas, but he obeyed the World Honored One's command to go to Vimalakirti and ask about his illness. "To the single room that's been swept repeatedly." Vimalakirti had cleared everything out of his room, just leaving his bench. When Manjusri arrived, he asked about the Dharma gate of nonduality, so Hsueh Tou says, "He asks about the gate of nonduality."

"Then Vimalakirti leans and falls." Vimalakirti's mouth was bent into a frown. Followers of Ch'an these days say that his speechlessness was the leaning and falling. But don't mistakenly go by the zero point of the scale.

Pushing you up onto a ten thousand fathom cliff, Hsueh Tou then says, "He doesn't lean and fall." With one hand he lifts up, with one hand he pushes down. Hsueh Tou has this kind of skill, and the way he uses it is sharp and clear. This line versifies his own previous comment, "What did Vimalakirti say?"

"The golden-haired lion has no place to look." It was not only this way at that time, but it's this way right now. Do you see old Vimalakirti? Even if the whole world, the mountains, rivers, grasses, trees, and forests all turned into a golden-haired lion (for you to ride, as does Manjusri), you still wouldn't be able to find him.

TRANSLATORS' NOTES

a. The image of a dog which, hit with a clod of dirt thrown by a man, ignores the man and chases the clod in anger, is found in the *Kasyapa-parivarta* (the old *Maharatnakuta* scripture); it symbolizes those who are afraid of the delights of the senses and seek deliverance in solitude and quiet—they never really become free because they are dependent on solitude and quiet, becoming every bit as much, and even more, miserable and confused as before when they again come in contact with the hustle and bustle of ordinary life.

b. Vimalakirti's show of disease is the setting of the *Vimalakirtinirdesa*, the scripture spoken by Vimalakirti, a major Mahayana Buddhist scripture; at first Shakyamuni directed his great disciples one by one to go to ask after Vimalakirti, but each explained how in the past Vimalakirti had criticized their practices and shattered their views, demolishing the dualistic (*samsara* vs. *nirvana*) standpoint of Hinayana (Lesser Vehicle) Buddhism (which is also symbolized by the 'dog chasing a clod' image of asceticism noted above). So after the disciples begged off, Shakyamuni then sent a host of bodhisattvas led by Manjusri to inquire after Vimalakirti; the latter took this opportunity to edify the bodhisattvas, and the discussion of nonduality, as well as miraculous displays and profound teachings by Vimalakirti, ensued.

EIGHTY-FIFTH CASE

The Hermit of T'ung Feng Makes a Tiger's Roar

POINTER

To hold the world fast without the slightest leak, so that all the people in the world lose their points and become tongue-tied—this is the true imperative for patchrobed monks.

To release a light from one's forehead that shines through the four quarters—this is the adamantine eye of patchrobed monks.

To touch iron and turn it into gold, to touch gold and turn it into iron, to suddenly capture and suddenly release—this is the staff of patchrobed monks.

To cut off the tongues of everyone in the world so that there's no place for them to breathe out, to make them fall back three thousand miles—this is the mettle of patchrobed monks.

But tell me, when one is not this way at all, who is he? To test I cite this to see.

CASE

A monk came to the place of the hermit of T'ung Feng and asked, "If you suddenly encountered a tiger here, what then?"[1] The hermit made a tiger's roar.[2] The monk then made a gesture of fright.[3] The hermit laughed aloud.[4] The monk said, "You old thief!"[5] The hermit said, "What can you do about me?"[6] The monk gave up.[7]

Hsueh Tou said, "This is all right, but these two wicked thieves only knew how to cover their ears to steal the bell."[8]

NOTES

1. The fellow is an expert at playing with shadows. Within the nest of weeds, there's one or a half.

548

2. He adds error to error. Nevertheless he does have teeth and claws. They are born together and die together. "Hearing the words, you should understand the source."
3. Two fellows playing with a mud ball. The monk saw his opportunity and acted. He seems to be right, but in reality he isn't.
4. This still amounts to something. In his laugh there's a sword. He can let go and he can also gather in.
5. You too must see through this. The monk has been defeated. The two of them both let go.
6. I would slap him across the ear. Too bad the monk let him go. He adds another layer of frost on top of snow.
7. Thus he was stopped. Neither of them understood. Heavens! Heavens!
8. The words are still in our ears. They have been censured by Hsueh Tou. But tell me, at that time, how should they have acted to avoid Hsueh Tou's criticism? No patchrobed monk in the world arrives.

COMMENTARY

The Ta Hsiung lineage (of Pai Chang Huai Hai) produced four hermits: Ta Mei,[a] Pai Yun, Hu Ch'i, and T'ung Feng.

Look at how those two men had such knowing eyes and capable hands. Tell me, where is the place that's difficult to understand? Though produced to meet the situation, the Ancients' one device, one object, one word, one phrase, are naturally leaping with life, since their eyes are perspicacious and true. Hsueh Tou picked this case to make people know wrong from right and discern gain and loss. Nevertheless, from his standpoint as a man who has arrived, though it's handled in terms of gain and loss, after all there is no gain or loss. If you view those Ancients in terms of gain and loss, you miss the point entirely. People of the present day must each comprehend the place where there's no gain or loss. If you only apply your mind to picking and choosing among words and phrases, when will you ever be done?

Haven't you heard how Great Master Yun Men said, "Foot-travellers, don't just wander over the country idly, just wanting to pick up and hold onto idle words. As soon as some old teacher's mouth moves, you immediately ask about Ch'an and ask about Tao, ask about transcendance and accommodation, ask about how and what. You make great volumes of commentaries which you stuff into your bellies, pondering and calculating. Wherever you go you put your heads together by the stove in threes and fives, babbling on and on. These, you say, are words of eloquence; these, words in reference to the self; these, words in reference to things; these, words from within the essence. You try to comprehend the old fathers and mothers of your house. Once you have gobbled down your meal, you only speak of dreams and say, 'I have understood the Buddha Dharma.' You should know that if you go foot-travelling this way, you will never be done."

When the Ancients briefly picked it up and played with it, how could there be such views as victory and defeat, gain and loss, or right and wrong?

T'ung Feng had seen Lin Chi. At the time of the story he had built a hut deep in the mountains. This monk came there and asked, "If you suddenly encountered a tiger here, what then?" Feng then made a tiger's roar; he rightly went to the thing to act. This monk too knew how to meet error with error, so he made a gesture of fright. When the hermit laughed aloud, the monk said, "You old thief!" Feng said, "What can you do about me?" This is all right, but neither of them understood. From ancient times on down, they've met with other people's criticism. Thus Hsueh Tou said, "This is all right, but these two wicked thieves only knew how to cover their ears to steal the bell." Though both of them were thieves, nevertheless they didn't take the opportunity to act; hence, they were covering their own ears to steal the bell. With these two Elders, it's as though they set up battle lines of a million troops, but only struggled over the broom (for sweeping up casualties).

To discuss this matter, it is necessary to have the ability to kill people without blinking an eye. If you always let go and never capture, if you always kill and never bring to life, you won't avoid the scornful laughter of others. Although this is so, these Ancients still didn't have so many concerns. Observe how they both saw their opportunity and acted. Wu Tsu spoke of the concentration of supernatural powers at play, the concentration of the torch of wisdom, and the concentration of the King of Adornment. It's just that people of later times don't have their feet on the ground; they just go criticize the An-

cients and say there is gain and loss. Some say that the hermit
clearly lost the advantage, but this has nothing to do with it.

Hsueh Tou said, "When these two men met, it was all letting go." When the monk said, "If you suddenly encountered a
tiger here, then what?" and Feng made a tiger's roar, this was
letting go. And when he said, "What can you do about me?"
this too was letting go. In every instance they fell into the
secondary level of activity. Hsueh Tou said, "If you want to
act, then act." People these days hear such talk and say that at
the time the hermit should have carried out the imperative for
the monk. But you shouldn't blindly punish and beat the hermit.

As for Te Shan immediately hitting people when they came
in through the gate, and Lin Chi immediately shouting at
people when they came in through the gate—tell me, what was
the intent of these Ancients? In the end Hsueh Tou makes his
verse just like this. But tell me, in the end, how will you avoid
"covering your own ears to steal the bell"?

VERSE

If you don't grab it when you see it,
　　You've stumbled by. It's already a thousand, ten thousand
　　miles away.
You'll think about it a thousand miles away.
　　Regretting that you weren't careful from the first.
　　Heavens! Heavens!
Fine stripes—
　　Take what's coming to you and get out, Reverend. What
　　could he do—he didn't know to act.
But he hasn't got claws and teeth.
　　I only fear that his use of them will be ignorant. I'll talk to
　　you when your claws and teeth are ready.
Haven't you seen the sudden encounter on Mt. Ta Hsiung?
　　If you have a rule, go by the rule; if you have no rule, go by
　　the example.
The vast sound and light shakes the earth—
　　This tiger, after all, goes on this way. Still he amounts to
　　something. How many sons are powerful men?

Do great men of power see or not?
> Hsueh Tou is so kind. If you can open your eyes, you can be born together and die together. Hsueh Tou is creating complications.

They take the tiger's tail and grab the tiger's whiskers.
> How will you take it when it suddenly appears? All the patchrobed monks in the world are taken in here. If one suddenly comes forth, I'd challenge him. I'm making you turn around and spew out your breath. Ha! I hit, saying, "Why didn't you say, 'You old thief!'?"

COMMENTARY

"If you don't grab it when you see it, / You'll think about it a thousand miles away." Just at the point of danger, the monk couldn't use it at all; when the hermit said, "What can you do about me?" the monk should have given him some of his own provisions. If at that time he had been able to show his skill, the hermit would have had to have a last word. Both men only knew how to let go; they couldn't gather in. "If you don't grab it when you see it" is already white clouds for ten thousand miles; why did he go on to say, "You'll think about it a thousand miles away"?

"Fine stripes— / But he hasn't got claws and teeth." This is so, but a tiger also knows how to conceal his teeth and hide his claws. What could he do, though—he didn't know how to bite people.

"Haven't you seen the sudden encounter on Mt. Ta Hsiung? / The vast sound and light shakes the earth." One day Pai Chang asked Huang Po, "Where are you coming from?" Po said, "From down the mountain." Chang said, "See any tigers?" Po then made a tiger's roar. Chang took the axe at his side and made the gesture of chopping. Po held it fast and slapped him. That evening Chang went up into the hall and said, "Down Ta Hsiung Mountain there's a tiger; all of you must watch out for him when you're going and coming. Today I myself have been bitten by him."

Later Kuei Shan asked Yang Shan, "What about Huang Po's tiger story?" Yang said, "What is your esteemed opinion,

Teacher?" Kuei Shan said, "At the time Pai Chang should have chopped him to death with one blow; how did it come to this?" Yang Shan said, "Not so." Kuei Shan said, "What about it then?" Yang Shan said, "Not only did he ride the tiger's head, but he also knew how to take the tiger's tail." Kuei Shan said, "You do indeed have some precipitous phrases, Chi." Hsueh Tou draws on this to illumine the main case.

"The vast sound and light shakes the earth." This bit transforms freely. Hsueh Tou wants to have a road to show himself within the words. "Do great men of power see or not?" Do you see? "They take the tiger's tail and grab the tiger's whiskers." Here again this must be one's own. Even if you take the tiger's tail and grab the tiger's whiskers, you won't avoid me instantly piercing your nostrils.

TRANSLATORS' NOTES

a. Ta Hsiung was the name of the mountain on which Ch'an Master Pai Chang Huai Hai lived and taught in the eighth and ninth centuries A.D. It was known as Pai Chang because of its precipitous heights, and the master Huai Hai was also known by that name, according to custom. Ta Mei was actually an early successor of Ma Tsu Tao I, Pai Chang's teacher; the hermit of T'ung Feng was a successor of Lin Chi, who succeeded to Huang Po, Pai Chang's great disciple. Four of Lin Chi's successors were hermits.

Yun Men's Kitchen Pantry and Main Gate

POINTER

He holds the world fast without the slightest leak; he cuts off the myriad flows without keeping a drop. Open your mouth and you're wrong; hesitate in thought and you miss. But tell me, what is the barrier-penetrating eye? To test, I cite this to see:

CASE

Yun Men imparted some words saying, "Everyone has a light;[1] when you look at it, you don't see it and it's dark and dim.[2] What is everybody's light?"[3]

He himself answered on their behalf, "The kitchen pantry and the main gate."[4] He also said, "A good thing isn't as good as nothing."[5]

NOTES

1. Black lacquer buckets.
2. When you look, you're blinded.
3. Mountains are mountains, rivers are rivers. Washing black ink in a bucket of lacquer.
4. He is very kind, but why is he creating complications?
5. He himself knew that he had only gotten halfway there; still, this amounts to something.

COMMENTARY

In his room Yun Men imparted some words to teach people: "All of you—right where you stand, each and every one of you

554

has a beam of light shining continuously, now as of old, far removed from seeing or knowing. Though it's a light, when you're asked about it you don't understand—isn't it dark and dim?" For twenty years he handed down this lesson, but there was never anyone who understood his meaning.

Later Hsiang Lin asked Yun Men to speak on their behalf. Men said, "The kitchen pantry and the main gate." He also said, "A good thing isn't as good as nothing." Usually what he said in place of others was just a single sentence; why then are there two here? The first sentence barely opens a road for you to let you see. If you're for real, as soon as you hear it mentioned, you get right up and go. Yun Men feared people would get stuck here, so he also said, "A good thing is not as good as nothing." As before, he's swept it away for you.

As soon as they hear you mention "light," people these days immediately put a glare in their eyes and say, "Where is the kitchen pantry? Where is the main gate?" But this has nothing to do with it. Thus it is said, "Perceive the meaning on the hook; don't abide by the zero point of the scale." This matter is not in the eye or in the environment. To begin to understand you must cut off knowing and seeing, forget gain and loss, and become purified, naked, and perfectly at ease; each and every one must investigate on his own.

Yun Men said, "You come and go by daylight; you distinguish people by daylight. Suddenly it's midnight, and there's no sun, moon, or lamplight. If it's some place you've been to, then of course it's possible; in a place you have never been, can you even manage to get hold of something?"

(Shih T'ou's) *Merging of Difference and Sameness* says,

> *Right within light there's darkness,*
> *But don't see it as darkness:*
> *Right within darkness there's light,*
> *But don't meet it as light.*

If you cut off light and darkness, tell me, what is it? Thus it is said, "The mind flower emits light, shining on all the lands in the ten directions." P'an Shan said, "Light isn't shining on objects, nor do the objects exist. Light and objects both forgotten, then what is this?" Also it was said,

*This very seeing and hearing is not seeing and hear-
ing—*
*But there's no other sound and form that can be
offered to you.*
*Here, if you can understand that there's nothing at
all,*
You are free to separate, or not, essence and action.

Just understand Yun Men's final statement thoroughly, then
you can go back to the former one to roam at play. But ultimately, you do not make a living there. The ancient Vimalakirti said, "All things are established on a non-abiding
basis." You mustn't go here to play with lights and shadows
and give play to your spirit. Nor will it do to make up an
understanding in terms of nothingness. An Ancient said, "Better you should give rise to a view of existence as big as Mt.
Sumeru, than that you produce a view of nothingness as small
as a mustard seed." People of the (lesser) two vehicles[a] often
fall onesidedly into this view.

VERSE

Spontaneously shining, ranged in the solitary light.
    The myriad forms and images. Guest and host inter-
    mingle. He snaps your nostrils around. What are you do-
    ing, blind men?
He opens a route for you.
    Why only one route? Ten suns are shining side by side. He
    has managed to set down one route.
Flowers fall, the tree has no shadow—
    What end is there to creating complications? Where will
    you seek it? He fills a black lacquer bucket with black
    ink.
When looking, who doesn't see?
    Blind! You shouldn't always hold onto fences and grope
    along walls. Two blind men, three blind men . . . .
Seeing or not seeing—
    Both ends are cut off. Blind!

Riding backwards on an ox, entering the Buddha shrine.
Inside the main gate he joins his palms. Give me back the
story. I hit, saying, "Where has he gone?" Hsueh Tou too
is just making his living inside the ghost cave. Do you
understand? At midnight the sun comes out, at noonday
the midnight watch is sounded.

COMMENTARY

"Spontaneously shining, ranged in the solitary light." Originally, right where you stand, there's this beam of light; it's just
that your use of it is dark. That's why Great Master Yun Men
set out this light for you right in front of your faces. But say,
what is everyone's light? "The kitchen pantry and the main
gate." This is where Yun Men arrays the solitary light. P'an
Shan said, "The mind-moon is solitary and full; its light engulfs myriad forms." This is the true, eternal, unique revela-
tion.

Afterwards "He opens a route for you." Yun Men still feared
that people would become attached to "The kitchen pantry,
the main gate." Conceding for the moment the kitchen pantry,
when the morning flowers fall and the tree has no shadow,
when the sun has gone down and the moon goes dark and all of
heaven and earth is black vastness—do you still see? "When
looking, who doesn't see?" Tell me, who is it that doesn't see?
Here, where "right within light there's darkness" and "right
within darkness there's light," both are "like a step forward
and a step backward." You must see for yourself.

Hsueh Tou says, "Seeing or not seeing," or versifies "A good
thing isn't as good as nothing." Merged with seeing, still you
don't see; merged with illumination, still you don't understand.

"Riding backwards on an ox, entering the Buddha shrine."
He's gone into the black lacquer bucket. You must personally
ride the ox into the Buddha shrine to see what it is that he's
saying.

TRANSLATORS' NOTES

a. The two vehicles refer to Buddhist disciples and self-enlightened
    sages, who strive only for the extinction of passion and personal
    suffering; they only realize the emptiness of ego and do not realize
    the emptiness of things as identical to the things themselves.
    They are apt to fall into the empty quiescence of subjective noth-
    ingness, intoxicated by trance. Bodhisattvas, however, realizing
    that existence itself is empty and not made so by annihilation, do
    not fear life or seek death, and arouse great kindness and compas-
    sion towards living beings, resolving that they all be liberated. If
    one clings to the idea of nothingness, this compassion is impossi-
    ble.

Medicine and Disease Subdue Each Other

POINTER

A clear-eyed fellow has no nest: sometimes on the summit of the solitary peak weeds grow in profusion; sometimes he's naked and free in the bustling marketplace. Suddenly he appears as an angry titan with three heads and six arms; suddenly as Sun Face or Moon Face Buddha he releases the light of all-embracing mercy. In a single atom he manifests all physical forms; to save people according to their type, he mixes with mud and water. If suddenly he releases an opening upwards, not even the Buddha's eye could see him; even if a thousand sages appeared, they too would have to fall back three thousand miles. Is there anyone with the same attainment and same realization? To test, I cite this to see.

CASE

Yun Men, teaching his community, said, "Medicine and disease subdue each other:[1] the whole earth is medicine;[2] what is your self?"[3]

NOTES

1. A compounded form cannot be grasped.
2. Bitter gourd is bitter to the root. He's put it over to one side.
3. Sweet melon is sweet to the stem. Where did he get this news?

COMMENTARY

Yun Men said, "Medicine and disease subdue each other: the whole earth is medicine; what is your self?" Do all of you have

559

a way to get out? Twenty-four hours a day, concentrate on "towering like a mile-high wall." Te Shan's blows fall like rain, Lin Chi's shouts roll like thunder—putting this aside for the moment, Shakymuni is himself Shakyamuni and Maitreya is himself Maitreya. Those who don't know what it comes down to frequently understand by calling it "medicine and disease merging with each other." For forty-nine years, in more than three hundred assemblies, the World Honored One adapted to potential to set up the teachings—all of this was giving medicine in accordance with the disease, like exchanging sweet fruit for bitter gourds. Having purified your active faculties, he made you clean and free.

"The whole earth is medicine." Where will you sink your teeth into this? If you can sink your teeth in, I'll grant that you have a place to turn around and show some life; then you see Yun Men in person. If you look around and hesitate, you won't be able to get your teeth into it; Yun Men is the one under your feet.

"Medicine and disease subdue each other." This is just an ordinary proposition. If you cling to existence, he speaks of nonexistence for you; if you are attached to nonexistence, he speaks of existence for you. If you are attached to neither existence nor nonexistence, he manifests the sixteen-foot golden body for you in a pile of crap and rubbish, appearing and disappearing.

Right now this whole great earth is a profuse array of myriad forms, up to and including one's own self. At once it's medicine—at such a time, what will you call your self? If you only call it medicine, even by the time Maitreya Buddha is born down here, you still won't have seen Yun Men even in dreams. Ultimately, how is it? "Perceive the meaning on the hook; don't stick by the zero point of the scale."

One day Manjusri ordered Sudhana to pick medicinal herbs. He said, "If there is something that is not medicine, bring it to me." Sudhana searched all over, but there was nothing that was not medicine. So he went back and told Manjusri, "There is nothing that is not medicine." Manjusri said, "Gather something that is medicine." Sudhana then picked up a blade of grass and handed it to Manjusri. Manjusri held it up and showed it to the assembly, saying, "This medicine can kill people and it can also bring people to life."

This talk of medicine and disease subduing each other is extremely difficult to see. Yun Men often used it in his room to guide people. One day Elder Chin O called on Hsueh Tou. Chin O was an adept, an honorable worthy of the Yun Men succession. They discussed this statement "medicine and disease subdue each other" all night until dawn before they were finally able to exhaust its excellence. At this point no learned interpretations, thought or judgment can be employed. Afterwards, Hsueh Tou made a verse to see him off which said,

> *Medicine and disease subdue each other—most difficult to see;*
> *The ten thousand locked gates indeed have no starting point.*
> *Wayfarer Chin O came calling;*
> *In one night we exhausted the waves of the ocean of learning.*

Hsueh Tou's subsequent verse is most effective. Is his meaning in the host or in the guest? You must see for yourself.

VERSE

The whole earth is medicine:
    Who would you have discern the point? Scattering sand and dirt. Put it on a high shelf.

Why have Ancients and moderns been so mistaken?
    There's an echo in the words. With one brush stroke they're all blotted out.

I don't make the carriage behind closed doors—
    Great Hsueh Tou uses all his strength to help the assembly, but misfortune comes forth from his own door. In the calm vastness, not a hair is hanging. Who has any spare time? He is making a living in a ghost cave.

The road through is naturally quiet and empty.
    Set foot on it and you enter the weeds. When you get on the horse, you'll see the road. He picks it up freely, undeniably outstanding.

Wrong! Wrong!
    Twin swords fly through space. A single arrow fells two eagles.

*Though they be high as the sky, your nostrils have still been
　　pierced.*
　　Your head has fallen. I hit, saying, "They've been
　　pierced!"

COMMENTARY

"The whole earth is medicine: / Why have Ancients and moderns been so mistaken?" From ancient times till now those of
you who have understood by calling it medicine have instantly
gone wrong. Hsueh Tou said, "There's a kind of person who
doesn't know how to cut off Ta Mei's footsteps, but merely
says that (Ta Mei) was in too much of a hurry to go."[a] Hsueh
Tou knew how to cut off Yun Men's footsteps.

Since this one line of his had thrown everyone in the world
into confusion, Yun Men said, "When my staff is waves, you
may go freely in all directions; when the whole earth is waves,
I'll watch to see if you float or sink."

"I don't make the carriage behind closed doors—/The road
through is naturally quiet and empty." Hsueh Tou speaks to
open up a road for you: "If you build your carriage behind
closed doors, and you bring it out the gate and it fits the ruts,
what has this accomplished? I am not building the carriage
behind closed doors here. When I go out the door, naturally it's
quiet and empty." Here Hsueh Tou reveals a slight crack to let
people see.

Still hurrying on, Hsueh Tou then says, "Wrong! Wrong!"
Both Yun Men's former statement and his latter statement are
wrong. Who would know that Hsueh Tou's opening up a road
is also wrong? Since your nostrils are as high as the sky, why do
they get pierced anyway? Do you want to understand? Then
immerse yourself in this for thirty years. If you have a staff, I'll
give you a staff; if you have no staff, you won't avoid having
your nostrils pierced by others.

TRANSLATORS' NOTES

a.　When Ta Mei was about to die he said, "Coming, there is nothing
　　to look to; going, there is nothing to pursue." Happening to hear

the cry of a squirrel, he said, "It's just this thing, not anything else. Keep it well—I am going to go." Later Hsueh Tou said of this, "This fellow was sloppy in life and fat-headed in death. 'Just this thing, not anything else'—what thing is this? Is there anything to impart, or not? Some people do not know how to cut off Ta Mei's footsteps, and merely say that he was in too much of a hurry to be on his way."

Hsuan Sha's Guiding and Aiding Living Beings

POINTER

The established methods of our school are thus: they break two into three. For profound talk entering into principle, you too must be piercing and penetrating.

Taking charge of the situation, he hits home and smashes to pieces the golden chains[a] and the hidden barrier. He acts according to the imperative, so that he obliterates all tracks and traces.

Tell me, where is there confusion? For those who have the eye on their forehead, I bring this up to see.

CASE

Hsuan Sha, teaching the community, said, "The old adepts everywhere all speak of guiding and aiding living beings.[1] Supposing they encountered three kinds of sick person, how would they guide them?[2] With a blind person, they could pick up the gavel or raise the whisk, but he wouldn't see.[3] With a deaf person, he wouldn't hear the point of words.[4] With a mute person, if they had him speak, he wouldn't be able to speak.[5] But how would they guide such people? If they couldn't guide these people, then the Buddha Dharma has no effect."[6]

A monk asked Yun Men for instruction on this.[7] Yun Men said, "Bow."[8] The monk bowed and rose.[9] Yun Men poked at him with his staff; the monk drew back. Yun Men said, "You're not blind."[10] Then Yun Men called him closer; when the monk approached,[11] Men said, "You're not deaf."[12] Next Yun Men said, "Do you understand?"[13] The monk said, "I don't understand."[14] Yun Men said, "You're not mute."[15] At this the monk had an insight.[16]

NOTES

1. They set up their shops according to their capacities, according to whether their houses are rich or poor.
2. He is beating the weeds just to frighten the snakes. My mouth is agape, my eyes open wide. You must fall back three thousand miles.
3. Truly blind! This is guiding and aiding living beings. One doesn't have to be blind (not to see).
4. Truly deaf! This is guiding and aiding living beings. One doesn't have to be have to be deaf (not to hear). Who hasn't heard yet?
5. Truly mute! This is guiding and aiding living beings. One doesn't have to be mute (to be unable to speak). Who hasn't spoken yet?
6. How true these words are! I fold my hands and submit, having already accepted. I'll strike!
7. He wants everyone to know too. This is pertinent.
8. When the wind blows, the grasses bend. Bah!
9. This monk has broken the staff.
10. Truly blind! Better not say this monk is blind.
11. The second ladleful of foul water douses the monk. Avalokitesvara has come. At that time the monk should have given a shout.
12. Truly deaf. Better not say the monk is deaf.
13. Why doesn't Yun Men offer his own provisions? At that time the monk shouldn't have made a sound.
14. A doubled case. Heavens! Heavens!
15. Truly mute. His mouth is babbling. Better not say this monk is mute.
16. He draws his bow after the thief has gone. What bowl[b] is he looking for?

COMMENTARY

Hsuan Sha had investigated till he reached the point of eliminating all emotional defilement and conceptual thought, where he became purified and naked, free and unfettered; only thus could he speak this way. At this time, when (Ch'an flourished) and the various monasteries all looked to one another, Hsuan Sha would often teach his community by saying, "The old adepts, all over, all speak of guiding and aiding living beings. If they should encounter three kinds of sick person, how would they guide them? With a blind person, they could pick up the gavel or raise the whisk, but he wouldn't see. With a deaf person, he wouldn't hear the point of words. With a mute person, if they had him speak, he wouldn't be able to speak. So how would they teach such people? If they couldn't guide these people, then the Buddha Dharma has no effect." If you people right now understand this as being blind, deaf, and mute, you'll never be able to find it. Thus it is said, "Don't die in the words." To attain, you must understand Hsuan Sha's meaning.

Hsuan Sha often used this statement to guide people. There was a monk who had been with Hsuan Sha for a long time. One day, when Hsuan Sha went up into the hall, this monk asked, "Will you permit me to present a theory of the story of the three kinds of sick person, Teacher?" Hsuan Sha said, "Go ahead." The monk then bade farewell and left. Sha said, "Wrong! That's not it." Did this monk understand Hsuan Sha's meaning? Fa Yen subsequently said, "When I heard Master Ti Tsang tell about this monk I finally understood the story of the three kinds of sick person." If you say this monk didn't understand, then why would Fa Yen talk like this? If you say he did understand, then why did Hsuan Sha say "wrong"?

One day Ti Tsang said to Hsuan Sha, "Teacher, I hear you have a saying about three kinds of sick person—is this so or not?" Sha said, "It is so." Tsang said, "I have eyes, ears, nose, and tongue—how will you guide me, Teacher?" Hsuan Sha immediately stopped. If you can understand Hsuan Sha's meaning, how could it be in the words and phrases? Ti Tsang's understanding was naturally outstanding.

Later a monk took this story up with Yun Men. Men immediately understood his intentions and said, "Bow." The monk bowed and rose. Men poked at him with his staff, and the monk drew back. Men said, "You're not blind." Then Men called him closer. When the monk approached, Men said, "You're not deaf." Next he said, "Do you understand?" When the monk said, "I don't understand," Men said, "You're not mute." At this the monk attained insight. At the time, if the monk had been for real, when Yun Men told him to bow he would have immediately turned over his meditation seat. Then how could so many complications have appeared? But tell me, are Yun Men's understanding and Hsuan Sha's understanding the same or different? The understanding of those two men was the same.

Look at how the Ancients appeared and created millions of kinds of expedient methods. "The meaning is on the hook." How much exertion to make each and every one of today's people understand this one matter!

My late teacher Wu Tsu said, "One man can speak, though he doesn't understand; one man, though he understands, cannot speak. If these two men came calling, how would you be able to discriminate between them? If you can't distinguish these two, in fact you will be unable to free what is stuck and untie what is bound for people. If you can distinguish them, then as soon as you see them come through the gate, you put on your straw sandals and walk around several times within their bellies. If you still haven't awakened on your own, what bowl are you looking for?[b] Go away!"

Now you better not make your understanding in terms of blind, deaf, and mute. Thus it is said, "His eyes see forms as though blind, and his ears hear sounds as though deaf." Again, it was said,

> *Though it fills his eyes, he doesn't see form;*
> *Though it fills his ears, he doesn't hear sound—*
> *Manjusri is always covering his eyes,*
> *Avalokitesvara blocks his ears.*

At this point, only if your eyes see as though blind and your ears hear as though deaf will you be able to not be at odds with Hsuan Sha's meaning. Do all of you know where the blind, deaf, and mute fellows are at? Look closely at Hsueh Tou's verse, which says,

VERSE

Blind, deaf, mute—
> Already there before it's said. The three openings (eye, ear, mouth) are all illumined. It's already been made into one piece.

Soundless, without any adjustments to potentialities.
> Where will you search? Can you make any judgments? What have they got to do with it?

In the heavens, on earth—
>   With the correct principle, Hsueh Tou is on his own. I am
>   also thus.

Laughable, lamentable.
>   Laugh at what? Lament over what? Half light, half dark.

Li Lü can't discern the true form;
>   Blind man! A skillful craftsman leaves no traces. Truly
>   blind!

How can Shih K'uang recognize the mystic tune?
>   Deaf man! No reward has been established for the great
>   achievement. Truly deaf.

How can this compare to sitting alone beneath an empty win-
>   *dow?*
>   You must be this way to attain. Don't make your living in
>   a ghost cave. Instantly Hsueh Tou smashes the lacquer
>   bucket.

The leaves fall, the flowers bloom—each in its own time.
>   What time and season is it right now? You mustn't under-
>   stand it as unconcern. Today goes from morning to eve-
>   ning and tomorrow too goes from morning to evening.

Again Hsueh Tou said, "Do you understand or not?"
>   Again he speaks the words of the verse.

An iron hammer head with no hole.
>   Take what's coming to you and get out! Too bad—Hsueh
>   Tou let go, so I'll hit.

COMMENTARY

"Blind, deaf, mute— / Soundless, without any adjustments to
potentialities." All your seeing and not seeing, hearing and not
hearing, speaking and not speaking—Hsueh Tou has swept it
all away at once for you. In fact, views in terms of blindness,
deafness, and muteness, and calculations and judgments of
what's right to suit potentials are at once silenced and cut off;
none of them can be applied. This transcendental matter can be
called real blindness, real deafness, real muteness, without potentials and without adjustments.

"In the heavens, on earth— / Laughable, lamentable." Hsueh Tou lifts up with one hand and pushes down with one hand. But say, laugh at what? Lament over what? It's worth laughing joyously that this blindness is not really blind, that this deafness is not really deaf, that this muteness is not really mute. It's worth lamenting being clearly not blind, yet still being blind, being clearly not deaf, yet still being deaf, being clearly not mute, yet still being mute.

"Li Lü can't discern the true form." If you can't tell green from yellow or red from white, then you're really blind. Li Lü was a man of the time of the Yellow Emperor (third millennium B.C.); from a hundred paces away he could see the tip of the finest hair—his eyes were very clear. As the Yellow Emperor was crossing the Red River, he dropped a pearl down into the water; he ordered Li Lü to look for it, but he couldn't find it. He ordered Ch'i Hou to search for it, but he couldn't find it either. Finally he ordered Hsiang Wang to look, and he at last recovered it. Thus it was said, "Hsiang Wang's glory shone bright at all times; Li Lü's actions were like waves flooding the sky." Even Li Lü's eye can't discern the true form of this lofty place.

"How can Shih K'uang recognize the mystic tune?" In Chou times (first millennium B.C.) Duke Ching of Chin had a son (some say it was the music teacher of Duke P'ing of Chin) named Shih K'uang Tzu Yeh, who was well able to distinguish the five notes and six pitches. He could hear the sound of ants fighting on the other side of a mountain. At that time (the states of) Chin and Ch'u were contending for hegemony. Shih K'uang had but to strum his guitar and set the strings in motion in order to know that Ch'u would have no success in the war. Although he was like this, Hsueh Tou says that even he would be unable to recognize the mystic tune. People who, even though they are not deaf, are nonetheless still deaf, even if they were Shih K'uang, still couldn't recognize the mystic tune of this lofty place.

Hsueh Tou says, "I am not Li Lü, nor am I Shih K'uang— how can this compare to sitting alone beneath an empty window? The leaves fall, the flowers bloom—each in its own time." If you get to this realm, though you see, it's like not seeing; though you hear, it's like not hearing; though you speak, it's like not speaking. When hungry you eat and when tired you sleep. You let the leaves fall and the flowers bloom. When the leaves fall it's autumn; when the flowers bloom it's spring—each has its own time and season.

Having swept it clean for you, Hsueh Tou again puts down a single path and says, "Do you understand or not?" Hsueh Tou's strength is exhausted and his spirit wearied; he can just manage to say, "An iron hammer head with no (handle) hole." Be quick to set your eyes on this line; only then will you see. If you hesitate, you've missed it again.

(Master Yuan Wu held up his whisk and said,) Do you see? (Then he rapped once on the meditation seat and said,) Do you hear? (Then he came down from his seat and said,) Can you speak?

TRANSLATORS' NOTES

a. "Golden chains" is a classic Buddhist metaphor for the moral code or behavioral discipline, one of the three Buddhist studies. Though one renounces society to become a monk or nun, and is thus freed from the problems of secular life, one is said to be still bound by the "golden chains" of precepts. Attachment to precepts, pride in one's way of life, or belief in the efficacy of mere morality or ritual, is called a form of bondage in Buddhist teaching. In Ch'an this is extended to refer to the whole of the Buddhist teachings, to all sense of realization or attainment, attachment to holiness, which still must be transcended before one is really free. This is like the image of "gold dust in the eyes"; though gold (Buddha Dharma) is precious, gold chains still bind and gold dust still blinds: the qualities of Buddhahood are not to be set up as external objects of attainment.

b. The "bowl," from which one eats and drinks, symbolizes a line of reasoning or doctrine which one attempts to use to get the "nourishment" of understanding.

The Hands and Eyes of the Bodhisattva of Great Compassion

POINTER

If your whole body were an eye, you still wouldn't be able to see it. If your whole body were an ear, you still wouldn't be able to hear it. If your whole body were a mouth, you still wouldn't be able to speak of it. If your whole body were mind, you still wouldn't be able to perceive it.

Now leaving aside "whole body" for the moment, if suddenly you had no eyes, how would you see? Without ears, how would you hear? Without a mouth, how would you speak? Without a mind, how would you perceive? Here, if you can unfurl a single pathway, then you'd be a fellow student with the ancient Buddhas. But leaving aside "studying" for the moment, under whom would you study?

CASE

Yun Yen asked Tao Wu, "What does the Bodhisattva of Great Compassion use so many hands and eyes for?"[1]

Wu said, "It's like someone reaching back groping for a pillow in the middle of the night."[2]

Yen said, "I understand."[3]

Wu said, "How do you understand it?"[4]

Yen said, "All over the body are hands and eyes."[5]

Wu said, "You have said quite a bit there, but you've only said eighty percent of it."[6]

Yen said, "What do you say, Elder Brother?"[7]

Wu said, "Throughout the body are hands and eyes."[8]

NOTES

1. At that time Tao Wu should have given him some of his own

provisions. Why are you constantly running around? Why do you ask, Reverend?

2. Why didn't Tao Wu use his own provisions? One blind man leading a crowd of blind men.

3. He adds error to error. He's cheating everyone. There's no different dirt in the same hole. Yun Yen doesn't avoid running afoul of the point and cutting his hand.

4. Why bother to inquire further? He still had to ask; Yun Yen should be challenged.

5. What does this have to do with it? He's making his living in the ghost cave, washing a lump of dirt with mud.

6. There's no different dirt in the same hole. When the manservant sees the maidservant, he takes care. A leper drags along his companions.

7. How can one get it by accepting another's interpretation? Tao Wu too should be challenged.

8. The frog cannot leap out of the basket. He's snatched your eyes and made off with your tongue. Has he gotten a hundred percent or not? He's calling daddy poppa.

COMMENTARY

Yun Yen and Tao Wu were fellow students under Yao Shan. For forty years Yun Yen's side did not touch his mat. Yao Shan produced the whole Ts'ao-Tung school. There were three men with whom the Path of Dharma flourished: descended from Yun Yen was Tung Shan; descended from Tao Wu was Shih Shuang; and descended from Ch'uan Tzu was Chia Shan.

The Bodhisattva of Great Compassion (Avalokitesvara) has eighty-four thousand symbolic arms. Great Compassion has this many hands and eyes—do all of you? Pai Chang said, "All sayings and writings return to one's self."

Yun Yen often followed Tao Wu, to study and ask questions to settle his discernment with certainty. One day he asked him, "What does the Bodhisattva of Great Compassion use so many hands and eyes for?" Right at the start Tao Wu should have given him a blow of the staff across his back, to avoid so many complications appearing later. But Tao Wu was compassionate—he couldn't be like this. Instead, he gave Yun Yen an explanation of the reason, meaning to make him understand immediately. Instead (of hitting him) Tao Wu said, "It's like someone reaching back groping for a pillow in the middle of the night." Groping for a pillow in the depths of the night without any lamplight—tell me, where are the eyes?

Yun Yen immediately said, "I understand." Wu said, "How do you understand it?" Yen said, "All over the body are hands and eyes." Wu said, "You have said quite a bit there, but you've only said eighty percent of it." Yen said, "What do you say, Elder Brother?" Wu said, "Throughout the body are hands and eyes."

But say, is "all over the body" right, or is "throughout the body" right? Although they seem covered with mud, nevertheless they are bright and clean. People these days often make up emotional interpretations and say that "all over the body" is wrong, while "throughout the body" is right—they're merely chewing over the Ancients' words and phrases. They have died in the Ancients' words, far from realizing that the Ancients' meaning isn't in the words, and that all talk is used as something that can't be avoided. People these days add footnotes and set up patterns, saying that if one can penetrate this case, then this can be considered understanding enough to put an end to study. Groping with their hands over their bodies and over the lamp and the pillar, they all make a literal understanding of "throughout the body." If you understand this way, you degrade those Ancients quite a bit.

Thus it is said, "He studies the living phrase; he doesn't study the dead phrase." You must cut off emotional defilements and conceptual thinking, become clean and naked, free and unbound—only then will you be able to see this saying about Great Compassion.

Haven't you heard how Ts'ao Shan asked a monk, "How is it when (the Dharmakaya, the body of reality) is manifesting form in accordance with beings, like the moon (reflected) in the water?" The monk said, "Like an ass looking at a well." Shan said, "You have said quite a lot, but you've only said eighty percent of it." The monk said, "What do you say, Teacher?" Shan said, "It's like the well looking at the ass." This is the same meaning as the main case.

If you go to their words to see, you'll never be able to get out of Tao Wu's and Yun Yen's trap. Hsueh Tou, as an adept, no longer dies in the words; he walks right on Tao Wu's and Yun Yen's heads to versify, saying,

VERSE

"All over the body" is right—
> Four limbs, eight joints. This isn't yet the ultimate abode of patchrobed monks.

"Throughout the body" is right—
> There's half on the forehead. You're still in the nest. Blind!

Bringing it up is still a hundred thousand miles away.
> It won't do to let Tao Wu and Yun Yen go. Why only a hundred thousand miles?

Spreading its wings, the Roc soars over the clouds of the six compounds[b]—
> A tiny realm—I had thought it would be extraordinary. Check!

It propels the wind to beat against the waters of the four oceans.
> A bit of dust—I had thought no one in the world could cope with you. Wrong!

What speck of dust suddenly arises?
> Again he's adding footnotes for Ch'an people. Cut! He's picked it up, but where has he put it?

What wisp of hair hasn't stopped?
> Exceptional! Special! Blown away. Cut!

You don't see?
> Again this way.

The net of jewels hanging down in patterns; reflections upon reflections.
> So the great Hsueh Tou is doing this kind of thing—too bad! As before he's creating complications.

Where do the hands and eyes on the staff come from?
> Bah! He draws his bow after the thief has gone. I can't let you go. No one in the world has any way to show some life. Hsueh Tou has let go, but he still must take a beating. Again I hit and say, "Tell me, is mine right or is Hsueh Tou's right?"

Bah!
> After three or four shouts, then what?

COMMENTARY

"All over the body is right—/ Throughout the body is right."
Whether you say reaching back with the hand groping for a
pillow is it, or running the hand over the body is it, if you make
up such interpretations, you're doing nothing but making your
living in a ghost cave. In the end neither "all over the body" nor
"throughout the body" is right. If you want to see this story of
Great Compassion by means of emotional consciousness, in
fact you're still a hundred thousand miles away. Hsueh Tou
can play with a phrase—reviving, he says, "Bringing it up is
still a hundred thousand miles away."

In the subsequent lines Hsueh Tou versifies what was extraordinary about Tao Wu and Yun Yen, saying, "Spreading its
wings, the Roc soars over the clouds of the six compounds[a]—/
It propels the wind to beat against the waters of the four
oceans." The great Roc swallows dragons: with his wings he
sends the wind to beat against the waters; the waters part, then
the Roc captures the dragon and swallows it. Hsueh Tou is
saying that if you can propel the wind against the waves like
the great Roc, you would be very brave and strong indeed.

If such actions are viewed with the thousand hands and eyes
of the Bodhisattva of Great Compassion, it's just a little bit of
dust suddenly arising, or like a wisp of hair ceaselessly blown
by the wind. Hsueh Tou says, "If you take running the hands
over the body as the hands and eyes of Great Compassion, what
is this good for?" In fact this is just not enough for this story of
the Bodhisattva of Great Compassion. Thus, Hsueh Tou says,
"What speck of dust suddenly arises? / What wisp of hair hasn't
stopped?"

Hsueh Tou said of himself that an adept at once wipes away
his tracks. Nevertheless, at the end of the verse as usual he
broke down and gave a comparison—as before, he's still in the
cage. "You don't see? / The net of jewels hanging down in
patterns, reflections upon reflections." Hsueh Tou brings out
the clear jewels of Indra's net to use as patterns hanging down.
But tell me, where do the hands and eyes come to rest?

In the Hua Yen school they designate four Dharma realms:
first, the Dharma realm of principle, to explain one-flavor
equality; second, the Dharma realm of phenomena, to explain
that principle in its entirety becomes phenomena. Third, the

Dharma realm of principle and phenomena unobstructed, to explain how principle and phenomena merge without hindrance; fourth, the Dharma realm of no obstruction among phenomena, to explain that every phenomenon everywhere enters all phenomena, that all things everywhere embrace all things, all intermingling simultaneously without obstruction. Thus it is said, "As soon as a single speck of dust arises, the whole earth is contained therein; each atom contains boundless Dharma realms. That being so for each atom, it is so for all atoms."

As for the net of jewels; in front of Indra's Dharma Hall of Goodness, there's a net made of jewels. Hundreds of thousands of jewels are reflected in every individual jewel, and each jewel is reflected in hundreds of thousands of jewels. Center jewel and surrounding jewels reflect back and forth, multiplying and remultiplying the images endlessly. This is used to illustrate the Dharma realm of no obstruction among phenomena.

In the old days National Teacher Hsien Shou set up a demonstration using mirrors and a lamp. He placed ten mirrors around the circumference (of a room) and put a lamp in the center. If you observed any one mirror, you saw nine mirrors mirroring the lamp, mirrors and lamp all appearing equally and perfectly clearly.

Thus when the World Honored One first achieved true enlightenment, without leaving the site of enlightenment he ascended into all the heavens of the thirty-three celestial kingdoms, and at nine gatherings in seven places he expounded the Hua Yen scripture.

Hsueh Tou uses Indra's jewel net to impart the teaching of the Dharma realm of no obstruction among phenomena. The six aspects[b] are very clear; that is, the all-inclusive, the separate, the sameness, the difference, the formation, and the disintegration. Raise one aspect and all six are included. Because living beings in their daily activities are unaware of it, Hsueh Tou raises the clear jewels of Indra's net hanging down in patterns to describe this saying about the Bodhisattva of Great Compassion. It's just like this: if you are well able, amidst the jewel net, to understand the staff and the marvellous functioning of supernatural powers going out and coming in unobstructed, then you can see the hands and eyes of the Bodhisattva. That's why Hsueh Tou says, "Where do the hands and eyes on the staff come from?" This is to make you attain realization at the staff and obtain fulfillment at a shout.

When Te Shan hit people as soon as they came in through the gate, when Lin Chi shouted at people as soon as they came in through the gate, tell me, where were the hands and eyes? And tell me, why did Hsueh Tou go on at the end to utter the word "Bah!"? Investigate!

TRANSLATORS' NOTES

a. The six compounds are the six senses—eye, ear, nose, tongue, body, and mind, and their respective sense-fields.
b. The six aspects of all things are defined in terms of the interdependent coproduction or relative coexistence of all things. The classic metaphor is of a house: the house represents the all-inclusive aspect, its beams and such represent the separate, or distinct aspect; since the beams, etc., join to form a house and nothing else, this is their aspect of sameness, but since they depend on each other as individual parts which are not the same, this is their aspect of difference. As they collectively create a house, this is the aspect of formation, but since each part has its own position and does not individually create anything, this is the aspect of disintegration. Put another way, one compound contains many elements or qualities; this is the all-inclusive aspect. The many qualities or elements are not one; this is the separate, or distinct aspect. Many functions or meanings are not at odds with each other; this is the aspect of sameness. From these many functions or meanings, interdependent co-production takes place; this is the aspect of formation. These conditions each abide in their own nature, without moving; this is the aspect of disintegration. (This explanation is from the section on Fa Yen Ch'an in the *Jen T'ien Yen Mu*, "Eye of Humans and Gods.")

Chih Men's Body of Wisdom

POINTER

Even the thousand sages[a] have not transmitted the single phrase before sound. The single thread right before us is perpetually unbroken. Purified and naked, free and unbound, hair dishevelled and ears alert—tell me, what about it? To test, I cite this to see.

CASE

A monk asked Chih Men, "What is the body of wisdom?"[1] Chih Men said, "An oyster swallowing the bright moon."[2]

The monk asked, "What is the function of wisdom?"[3] Chih Men said, "A rabbit getting pregnant."[4]

NOTES

1. Throughout the body there are no reflected images. It cuts off the tongues of everyone in the world. What's he using "body" for?
2. Leaving aside for the moment "the light engulfs myriad forms," what is the affair of the correct eye on the staff? The crooked does not conceal the straight. Chih Men is adding a layer of frost on snow.
3. Fall back three thousand miles! What does he want "function" for?
4. Danger! A bitter gourd is bitter to the root, a sweet melon is sweet to the stem. If you make your living in the shadows of the light, then you won't get out of Chih Men's nest. If there is someone who can come out, tell me, is this the body of wisdom or the function of wisdom? In essence this is adding mud to dirt.

COMMENTARY

When Chih Men said, "An oyster swallowing the bright moon" and "A rabbit getting pregnant," in both he used a mid-autumn sense; even so, the Ancient's meaning was not in the oyster or the rabbit. As Chih Men was a venerable adept in the congregation of Yun Men,[b] each of his phrases had to contain three phrases; that is, the phrase that contains heaven and earth, the phrase that cuts off the myriad streams, and the phrase that follows the waves. Moreover, without using any prearranged maneuvers, each of his phrases is spontaneously appropriate. Thus he went to the danger point to answer this monk's questions, showing a bit of his sharp point—he was undeniably extraordinary. Nevertheless, this ancient never played with the shadows of a light, he just pointed out a bit of a road for you to make you see.

This monk said, "What is the body of wisdom?" Chih Men said, "An oyster swallowing the bright moon." Oysters contain bright pearls: (it is said that) when the mid-autumn moon comes out, the oysters float to the surface, open their mouths, and swallow the moonlight; from the effects of this, pearls are produced. If there is moonlight in mid-autumn, the pearls are many; without a moon, the pearls are few.

The monk also asked, "What is the function of wisdom?" Chih Men said, "A rabbit getting pregnant." The meaning of this is no different. The rabbit belongs to (the female, negative principle) Yin (to which the moon also belongs); in mid-autumn when the moon comes out, the rabbits open their mouths and swallow its light, thus becoming pregnant. Here too, if there's moonlight the offspring are many; without a moon, they're few.

That Ancient's answer was free from so many concerns; he just made temporary use of these meanings to answer about the light of wisdom. Although his answer was this way, his meaning wasn't in the words and phrases. It's just that later people go to his words to make a living. Haven't you heard how P'an Shan said,

> *The mind-moon is solitary and full:*
> *Its light engulfs the myriad forms.*

The light is not shining on objects,
Nor do the objects exist—
Light and objects both forgotten,
Then what is this?

People these days just stare and call this the light: from their feelings they produce interpretations, driving spikes into empty space.

An Ancient said, "Day and night all of you people release a great light from the gates of your six senses; it shines through mountains, rivers, and the great earth. It's not only your eyes that release light—nose, tongue, body and mind also all release light." To get here you simply must clean up your six sense faculties so that you're without the slightest concern, purified and naked, free and unbound—only then will you see where this story is at. Hsueh Tou does his verse just this way:

VERSE

One piece of empty solidity, beyond saying and feeling;
    Stir your mind and you err, move your thoughts and
    you're obstructed. Not even Buddha's eye can catch sight
    of it.
From this humans and gods see Subhuti.
    Subhuti should be given thirty blows. Why make use of
    this old fellow? Even Subhuti has to fall back three
    thousand miles.
The oyster swallowing, the mysterious rabbit—deep, deep
        meaning:
    You'd have to be the man himself to understand. What
    intention did he have? What further need for "deep, deep
    meaning"?
Having been given to Ch'an people, it makes them fight and
        struggle.
    When shields and spears are already at rest, then there's
    great peace under heaven. Do you understand? I hit, say-
    ing, "How many blows can you take, Reverend?"

COMMENTARY

"One piece of empty solidity, beyond saying and feeling." With a single line, Hsueh Tou has versified it well: naturally he can see the Ancient's meaning. What is it that the six senses are brimming with? It's just this one mass, empty and bright, solid and quiescent. You don't need to go to heaven to look for it. You don't have to seek it from someone else. The perpetual light spontaneously appears before us: right here in this very place it towers up like a mile-high wall, beyond verbal appellation and mental sense.

Fa Yen's verse on perfect reality says,

> When reasoning is exhausted, saying and feeling are
>   forgotten;
> How could this be properly described?
> Wherever I go, the frosty night's moon
> Falls as it may on the valley ahead.
> The fruits are ripe and heavy with monkeys,
> The mountains go on so far it seems I've lost my
>   way.
> When I raise my head, there's a remnant of illumi-
>   nation left—
> Actually this is west of my dwelling place.

Thus it is said,

> Mind is the faculty, things are the objects;
> Both are like flaws on a mirror.
> When the defilement of objects is obliterated, the
>   light first appears.
> When mind and things are both forgotten, nature is
>   real.

It is also said,

> I've always lived in a three-section reed hut;
> In the spiritual light of the one Path, myriad objects
>   are at rest.
> Don't use right and wrong to judge me—
> Fleeting life and its rationalizations have nothing to
>   do with me.

These verses too make you see "One piece of empty solidity, beyond saying and feeling."

"From this humans and gods see Subhuti." Haven't you heard how Subhuti was sitting quietly on a cliff when all the gods showered him with flowers to praise him: the venerable Subhuti said, "Who is showering down these flowers in praise?" A god said, "I am Brahma." Subhuti said, "Why are you offering praise?" The god said, "I honor you for being good at expounding the transcendance of wisdom." Subhuti said, "I have never spoken a single word about wisdom; why offer praise?" The god said, "You didn't speak and I didn't hear—no speaking and no hearing is true wisdom," and again he caused the earth to tremble and flowers to shower. See how Subhuti expounded wisdom so well, without speaking of its body or its function. If at this you can see, then you can see Chih Men's saying, "An oyster swallowing the bright moon" and "A rabbit getting pregnant."

Though the Ancient's meaning was not in the spoken phrases, nevertheless in his answer there was a deep, deep meaning. This caused Hsueh Tou to say, "The oyster swallowing, the mysterious rabbit—deep, deep meaning." Here, "Having been given to Ch'an people, it makes them fight and struggle." The followers of Ch'an in the world have haggled over Chih Men's answers profusely and noisily; there's never been a single person who has even seen him in a dream. If you want to be a fellow student with Chih Men and Hsueh Tou, you must first set your eyes on it for yourself.

TRANSLATORS' NOTES

a.   In Chinese convention, multiples of ten represent infinite numbers; ten thousand especially is so used and really means "myriad." Hence "the thousand sages" means "all the sages."

b.   Chih Men was a successor of the Yun Men lineage in the third generation; his teacher was Yun Men's great disciple Hsiang Lin Teng Yuan.

Yen Kuan's Rhinoceros

POINTER

To transcend emotion, detach from views, remove bonds and dissolve sticking points, to uphold the fundamental vehicle of transcendence and support the treasury of the eye of the true Dharma, you must also respond equally in all ten directions, be crystal clear in all respects, and directly attain to such a realm. But tell me, are there any who attain alike, realize alike, die alike and live alike? To test, I cite this to see.

CASE

One day Yen Kuan called to his attendant, "Bring me my rhinoceros-horn fan."[1]

The attendant said, "The fan is broken."[2]

Yen Kuan said, "If the fan is broken, bring the rhinoceros back to me."[3]

The attendant had no reply.[4]

T'ou Tzu said, "I do not refuse to bring it out, but I fear the horn on its head will be imperfect."[5] Hsueh Tou commented, "I want an imperfect horn."[6]

Shih Shuang said, "If I return it to the Master, then I won't have it."[7] Hsueh Tou commented, "The rhino is still there."[8]

Tzu Fu drew a circle and wrote the word 'rhino' inside it.[9] Hsueh Tou commented, "Why did you not bring it out before?"[10]

Pao Fu said, "The Master is aged; he should ask someone else."[11] Hsueh Tou commented, "What a pity to have worked hard without accomplishing anything."[12]

NOTES

1. He creates quite a few complications. How can it compare with the fine scene here?

2. What a pity! What is he saying?
3. He's broken down quite a bit. Yu province is still all right; the worst suffering is in Korea. What does the master want with the rhinoceros?
4. After all he's a hammerhead without a hole. What a pity!
5. This seems to be like it, but nevertheless he has two heads and three faces. He is still speaking theoretically.
6. What is it good for? He adds error to error.
7. What is he saying? It's right under his nose.
8. Danger! He almost mistook it. Pull its head back!
9. Grass that's withered isn't worth bringing out. He's a fellow playing with a shadow.
10. He doesn't distinguish gold from brass. He too is a fellow in the weeds.
11. In an out of the way place he rebukes an official. What is he doing, avoiding hardship yet speaking of his suffering?
12. You yourself are included. It would be even better to give thirty blows of the staff. Clearly.

COMMENTARY

Yen Kuan one day called to his attendant, "Bring me my rhinoceros-horn fan." Although this matter does not lie in words, yet if you want to test someone's ordinary disposition and ability, still it is necessary to be able to use words in this way to show it. On the last day of the last month of your life, if you can find strength and be the Master, even when myriad visions appear in profusion, you can look upon them without being moved: this can be called accomplishment without accomplishment, effortless power.

Yen Kuan was Ch'an Master Chi An; he used to have a fan made of rhinoceros horn. At the time, how could Yen Kuan not have known that the fan was broken? He purposely asked the attendant, and the attendant said, "The fan is broken." Observe how that Ancient was always within It twenty-four hours a day, encountering It everywhere; Yen Kuan said, "If the fan is broken, bring the rhinoceros back to me." But tell me, what did he want with the rhinoceros? He just wanted to test the man to see whether or not he knew where it was at.

T'ou Tzu said, "I do not refuse to bring it out, but I fear the head's horn will be imperfect." Hsueh Tou said, "I want the imperfect horn." He too goes to the phrase to match wits.

Shih Shuang said, "If I return it to the Master, then I won't have it." Hsueh Tou says, "The rhino is still there."

Tzu Fu drew a circle and wrote the word "rhino" inside; because he had succeeded to Yang Shan, he always liked to use objects to teach people and illustrate this matter. Hsueh Tou says, "Why didn't you bring it out before?" He pierced his nostrils too.

Pao Fu said, "The Master is aged; he should ask someone else." These words are most appropriate; the preceding three quotes are after all easy to see, but the words of this one phrase have a profound meaning. Yet Hsueh Tou has broken them up too. When I was at Librarian Ch'ing's place in the old days, I understood the reasoning; he said, "The Master is old and senile; getting the head, he forgets the tail—before he sought the fan, now he seeks the rhinoceros; it is hard to attend to him, and therefore (Pao Fu) said, 'Better ask someone else.'" Hsueh Tou said, "What a pity to work hard without accomplishing anything."

All these were in the form of remarks: the Ancients saw through this matter, so though each was different, when they spoke forth, they hit the mark a hundred times out of a hundred, always having a way to show forth; each phrase does not lose the bloodline. People these days, when they are questioned, just make up theoretical judgments and comparisons; that is why I want people to chew on this twenty-four hours a day, making every drop of water a drop of ice, seeking the experience of enlightenment. See how Hsueh Tou versified it on one thread, saying,

VERSE

The rhinoceros-horn fan has long been in use,
   In summer, cool; in winter, warm. Everyone has it; why don't they know? Who has never used it?

But when asked, actually nobody knows.
   They know, but they don't understand. Better not fool people. And you shouldn't suspect anyone else.

The boundless pure breeze and the horn on the head,
> Where are they? If you do not understand in yourself, where will you understand? In the heavens and on earth. The horn has regrown. What is it? He rouses waves without wnd.

Just like the clouds and rain, when gone, are difficult to pursue.
> Heavens! Heavens! Still this is losing one's money and incurring punishment anyway.

Hsueh Tou also said, "If you want the pure breeze to return, and the horn to regrow,[1] I ask you Ch'an followers to each turn a word.[2] I ask you, since the fan is broken, return the rhinoceros to me."[3]

At that time a monk came forth and said, "Everyone, go meditate in the hall!"[4]

Hsueh Tou said, "I cast my hook fishing for whales, but caught a frog." Then he got down from the seat.[5]

NOTES *(cont'd.)*

1. Everyone has this fan: throughout the twenty-four hours of the day, they completely obtain its power; why do they not know at all when they are asked? Can you speak?
2. He has already spoken thrice. Yen Kuan is still alive.
3. There is yet one or a half. Bah! It would be better to overthrow his meditation seat.
4. He draws the bow after the thief has gone. He neither gets to the village nor reaches the shop.
5. He brought this about. He draws his bow after the thief is gone.

COMMENTARY

"The rhinoceros-horn fan has long been in use, / But when asked, actually nobody knows." Everyone has this fan, and throughout the twenty-four hours of the day is in complete possession of its power—why is it that when asked, no one knows where it's gone? The attendant, T'ou Tzu, all the way down to Pao Fu—neither do any of them know. But tell me, does Hsueh Tou know?

Have you not seen how when Wu Cho called on Manjusri, as they were drinking tea, Manjusri held up a crystal bowl and asked, "Do they have this in the South?" Wu Cho said, "No." Manjusri said, "What do they usually use to drink tea?" Wu Cho was speechless. If you know what this public case is about, then you will know that the rhinoceros-horn fan has a boundless pure breeze; you will also see the horn towering on the rhino's head.

The four old fellows speaking as they did were like the morning clouds and evening rain; once gone, they are difficult to pursue. Hsueh Tou also said, "If you want the pure breeze to return and the horn to regrow, I ask you Ch'an followers to each utter a turning word: I ask you, since the fan is broken, return the rhinoceros to me." At that moment a Ch'an follower came forth and said, "Everyone, go meditate in the hall!" This monk has usurped the Master's sceptre of authority. He certainly could speak, but he was only able to say eighty percent. If you want a hundred percent, then throw the meditation seat over for him. Now, you tell me, did this monk understand the rhinoceros or not? If he did not understand, yet he knew how to speak in this way; if he did understand, why did Hsueh Tou not approve of him? Why did he say, "I cast a hook fishing for whales, but only caught a frog."

Tell me, ultimately how is it? Everyone, there's nothing to worry about; try to hold it up to view.

The World Honored One Ascends the Seat

POINTER

One who can discern the tune as soon as the lute strings move is hard to find even in a thousand years. By releasing a hawk upon seeing a rabbit, at once the swiftest is caught. As for summing up all spoken words into a single phrase, gathering the universe into a single atom, dying the same and being born the same, piercing and penetrating in all ways, is there anyone who can stand witness? To test, I cite this to see.

CASE

One day the World Honored One ascended his seat.[1] Manjusri struck the gavel and said, "Clearly behold the Dharma of the King of Dharma; the Dharma of the King of Dharma is thus."[2] The World Honored One then got down off the seat.[3]

NOTES

1. Guest and host both lose. This is not the only instance of indulgence.
2. One son has intimately understood.
3. Sad man, do not speak to sad people; if you speak to sad people, you'll sadden them to death. Beating the drum, playing the lute, two masters in harmony.

COMMENTARY

Before the World Honored One had raised the flower,[a] already there was this scene. From the beginning at the Deer Park[b] to the end at the Hiranyavati River,[c] how many times did he use the jewel sword of the Diamond King? At that time, if among the crowd there had been someone with the spirit of a patch-robed monk who could transcend, he would have been able to avoid the final messy scene of raising the flower. While the World Honored One paused, he was confronted by Manjusri, and immediately got down from his seat. At that time, there was still this scene; Shakyamuni barred his door, Vimalakirti shut his mouth—both resemble this, and thus have already explained it. It is like the story of Su Tsung asking National Teacher Chung about making a seamless memorial tower,[d] and also like the story of the outsider asking Buddha, "I do not ask about the spoken or the unspoken."[e] Observe the behavior of those transcendent people; when did they ever enter a ghost cave for their subsistence? Some say that the meaning lies in the silence; some say it lies in the pause, that speech illumines what cannot be said, and speechlessness illumines what can be said—as Yung Chia said, "Speaking when silent, silent when speaking." But if you only understand in this way, then past, present, and future, for sixty aeons, you will still never have seen it even in dreams. If you can immediately and directly attain fulfillment, then you will no longer see that there is anything ordinary or holy—this Dharma is equanimous, it has no high or low. Every day you will walk hand in hand with all the Buddhas.

Finally, observe how Hsueh Tou naturally sees and produces it in verse:

VERSE

Among the assembled multitude of sages, if an adept had
     known,
          Better not slander old Shakyamuni. Leave it up to Lin Chi
          or Te Shan. Among a thousand or ten thousand, it's hard
          to find one or a half.
The command of the King of Dharma wouldn't have been like
     this.
          Those who run after him are as plentiful as hemp and
          millet. Three heads, two faces. Clearly. How many could
          there be who could reach here?

In the assembly, if there had been a "saindhava man,"
> It's hard to find a clever man in there. If Manjusri isn't an
> adept, you sure aren't.

What need for Manjusri to strike the gavel?
> What is the harm of going ahead and striking the gavel
> once? The second and third strokes are totally unneces-
> sary. How will you speak a phrase appropriate to the situ-
> ation? angerous!

COMMENTARY

"Among the assembled multitude of sages, if an adept had
known." The great mass of eighty thousand on Vulture Peak
all were ranked among the sages: Manjusri, Samantabhadra,
and so on, including Maitreya; master and companions were
assembled together—they had to be the skilled among the
skillful, the outstanding among the outstanding, before they
would know what he was getting at. What Hsueh Tou intends
to say is that among the multitude of sages, there was not a
single man who knew what is: if there had been an adept, then
he would have known what was not so. Why? Manjusri struck
the gavel and said, "Clearly behold the Dharma of the King of
Dharma; the Dharma of the King of Dharma is thus." Hsueh
Tou said, "The command of the King of Dharma is not like
this." Why so? At the time, if there had been in the assembly a
fellow with an eye on his forehead and a talisman at his side, he
would have seen all the way through before the World Honored
One had even ascended the seat; then what further need would
there be for Manjusri to strike the gavel?

The Nirvana Scripture says, "*Saindhava* is one name for
four actual things: one is salt, the second is water, the third is a
bowl, and the fourth is a horse. There was a wise attendant
who well understood the four meanings: if the king wanted to
wash, and needed *saindhava*, the attendant would then bring
him water; when he asked for it when eating, then he served
him salt; when the meal was done, he offered him a bowl to
drink hot water; and when he wanted to go out, he presented a
horse. He acted according to the king's intention without error;
clearly one must be a clever fellow to be able to do this."

When a monk asked Hsiang Yen, "What is the king asking for *saindhava?*" Hsiang Yen said, "Come over here." The monk went; Hsiang Yen said, "You make a total fool of others." He also asked Chao Chou, "What is the king asking for *saindhava?*" Chou got off his meditation seat, bent over and folded his hands. At this time if there had been a *"saindhava* man"* who could penetrate before the World Honored One had even ascended his seat, then he would have attained somewhat. The World Honored One yet ascended his seat, and then immediately got down; already he hadn't got to the point— how was it worth Manjusri's still striking the gavel? He un- avoidably made the World Honored One's sermon seem foolish. But tell me, where was it that he made a fool of him?

TRANSLATORS' NOTES

a. This refers to the oft-repeated story of the Buddha holding a flower up before a huge assembly, whereat Mahakasyapa smiled, the only one to understand the Buddha's message. In Ch'an tradition this represents the first "heart to heart transmission" of Ch'an in India.
b. Shakyamuni Buddha gave his first sermon at the Deer Park in Benares, to five ascetics with whom he had formerly associated.
c. Shakyamuni Buddha died by the Hiranyavati River.
d. See case 18.
e. See case 65.

Ta Kuang Does a Dance

CASE

A monk asked Ta Kuang, "Ch'ang Ch'ing said, 'Joyful praise on the occasion of a meal'—what was the essence of his meaning?"[1a]

Ta Kuang did a dance.[2] The monk bowed.[3] Kuang said, "What have you seen, that you bow?"[4] The monk did a dance.[5] Kuang said, "You wild fox spirit!"[6]

NOTES

1. The light shines again. This lacquer tub! It is unavoidable to doubt; without asking, you won't know.
2. Do not deceive people completely. He acts in the same way as (Chin Niu did) before.
3. He too acts this way; he's right, but I fear he's misunderstood.
4. He still should press him; it's necessary to be discriminating.
5. He draws a cat according to a model. After all he misunderstood. He's a fellow playing with a shadow.
6. This kindness is hard to requite. The Thirty-three Patriarchs only transmitted this.

COMMENTARY

The Twenty-eight Patriarchs in India and the Six Patriarchs in China only transmitted this little bit; but do you people know what it comes down to? If you know, you can avoid this error; if you do not know, as before you will only be wild fox spirits.[b]

Some say (Ta Kuang) wrenched around the other's nostrils to deceive the man; but if it were actually so, what principle would that amount to? Ta Kuang was well able to help others; in his phrases there is a road along which to get oneself out. In general, a teacher of the school must pull out the nails, draw out the pegs, remove the sticking points and untie the bonds for people; only then can he be called "a good friend."ᶜ

Ta Kuang did a dance, the monk bowed; in the end, the monk also did a dance, and Ta Kuang said, "You wild fox spirit!" This was not turning the monk over; after all, if you do not know the real point, and just do a dance, going on one after the other like this, when will you ever find rest? Ta Kuang said, "Wild fox spirit"—these words cut off Chin Niu, and are undeniably outstanding. That is why it is said, "He studies the living word, not the dead word." Hsueh Tou just likes his saying "You wild fox spirit!" That is the basis on which he produces his verse. But tell me, is this "wild fox spirit" the same as or different from "Tsang's head is white; Hai's head is black,"ᵈ "This lacquer bucket!"ᵉ or "Good monk!"? Just tell me, are these the same or different? Do you know? You meet him everywhere.

VERSE

The first arrow was still light, but the second arrow went
       deep:
       A hundred shots, a hundred hits. Where can you go to
       escape?
Who says yellow leaves are yellow gold?
       Yet they'll put an end to crying; but even if you can fool a
       child, it's of no use.
If the waves of Ts'ao Ch'i were alike,
       What limit is there to people playing with mud balls? He
       draws a cat according to a model. He lets out a single road.
Innumerable ordinary people would get bogged down.
       We meet a living man! He has entangled every patchrobed
       monk in the world, and makes them unable to get a hold;
       he entangles you too, and makes you unable to appear.

COMMENTARY

"The first arrow was still light, but the second arrow went deep." Ta Kuang's dance was the first arrow. He also said,

"This wild fox spirit!" This was the second arrow. This has been the tooth and nail since time immemorial.

"Who says yellow leaves are yellow gold?" Yang Shan said to his community, "You people should each turn back your light and reflect; do not memorize my words. Since beginningless aeons you have turned your backs on the light and plunged into darkness; the roots of your false conceptions are deep, and after all are hard to pull out all at once. That is why I temporarily set up expedient methods to take away your coarse discriminating consciousness; this is like using yellow leaves to stop a little child's crying." It is like exchanging sweet fruit for bitter gourd. The Ancients provisionally established expedient methods to help people; when their crying has stopped, yellow leaves are not gold.[f] When the World Honored One explained timely doctrines throughout his lifetime, these too were just talks to put an end to crying. "This wild fox!"—he just wanted to transmute the other's active discriminating consciousness; within (the process) there are provisional and real, there are also illumination and function; only thus can you see the grasp of the patchrobed monk there. If you can understand, you'll be like a tiger with folded wings.

"If the waves of Ts'ao Ch'i were alike."[g] If suddenly all the students in all quarters did a dance like this, and only acted like this, then innumerable ordinary people would get bogged down; how could they be saved?

TRANSLATORS' NOTES

a.   See case 74; reference to that case is made several times.
b.   As a term of scorn, "wild fox spirit" connotes fakery or show; "wild fox Ch'an" is an expression used to refer to empty pretense.
c.   *Shan chih shih*, a translation of Sanskrit *kalyanamitra*, which means a good or virtuous friend, refers to a spiritual guide, teacher, benefactor.
d.   See case 73.
e.   A lacquer bucket, or lacquer tub, means an ignoramus. The blackness of lacquer symbolizes ignorance, lack of enlightenment.
f.   That is, just as yellow leaves are used to placate a crying child by pretending they are gold trinkets, various teachings and tech-

niques are used to put an end to people's confusion and misery, though ultimately, as Te Shan said, there is nothing to give to people, no true doctrine.

g. By Hsueh Tou's time, all the living streams of Ch'an were descended from the Sixth Patriarch Hui Neng, who is also referred to by the name Ts'ao Ch'i after his dwelling place. Ts'ao Ch'i was a river; the temple where Hui Neng taught was built near its source in Shao Chou in the far south of China.

The Surangama Scripture's Not Seeing

POINTER

The one phrase before sound is not transmitted by a thousand sages; the single thread before our eyes is forever without a gap. Pure and naked, bare and clean, the White Ox on Open Ground.ª Eyes alert, ears alert, the golden-haired lion—leaving this aside for a moment, tell me, what is the White Ox on Open Ground?

CASE

The *Surangama* scripture says, "When I do not see, why do you not see my not seeing?[1] If you see my not seeing, naturally that is not the characteristic of not seeing.[2] If you don't see my not seeing,[3] it is naturally not a thing[4]—how could it not be you?"[5]

NOTES

1. Good news! What is the use of seeing? Old Shakyamuni has broken down quite a bit.
2. Bah! What leisure time is there? You shouldn't tell me to have two heads and three faces.
3. Where are you going? It's like driving a nail into an iron spike. Bah!
4. He pushes down the ox's head to make it eat grass. What further verbal sound and form is there to speak of?
5. To say you or me is totally beside the point. Striking, I say, "Do you see old Shakyamuni?"

COMMENTARY

In the *Surangama* scripture it says, "When I don't see, why don't you see my not seeing? If you see my not seeing, naturally that is not the characteristic of not seeing. If you don't see my not seeing, it is naturally not a thing; how could it not be you?" Hsueh Tou here does not quote the entire passage of the scripture; if it is quoted in full, then it can be seen. The scripture says,[b] "If seeing were a thing, then you could also see my sight. If seeing alike were called seeing my (seeing), when I don't see, why don't you see my not seeing? If you see my not seeing, naturally that is not the characteristic of not seeing. If you don't see my not seeing, naturally it is not a thing; how could it not be you?" The words are many, and I won't record them. Ananda intended to say, "The lamps and pillars in the world all can be given names; I also want the World Honored One to point out this subtle spiritual fundamental illumination—what can you call it, to let me see the Buddha's intent?" The World Honored One says, "I see the incense stand." Ananda says, "I also see the incense stand; then this is the Buddha's sight." The World Honored One says, "When I see the incense stand, then that can be known; when I do not see the incense stand, then how will you see?" Ananda says, "When I don't see the incense stand, then this is seeing the Buddha." The Buddha says, "If I say I don't see, this is my own knowledge; when you say you don't see, this is your own knowledge—where another doesn't see, how can you know?" The ancients said that when you get here, you can only know for yourself; you can't explain to others. Just as the World Honored One said, "When I do not see, why don't you see my not seeing? If you see my not seeing, naturally that is not the characteristic of not seeing. If you do not see my not seeing, naturally it is not a thing; how could it not be you?" If you say you acknowledge sight as an existent thing, you are not yet able to wipe away the traces. "When I don't see" is like the antelope with his horns hung up—all echo of sound, traces of tracks, all breath is utterly gone; where will you turn to search for him? The sense of the scripture is total indulgence in the beginning and total restraint in the end. Hsueh Tou goes beyond the eye of the scriptural teachings to versify: he neither eulogizes things, nor seeing or not seeing; he just eulogizes seeing Buddha.

VERSE

"The Whole Elephant" or "The Whole Ox"—as blinding
   cataracts, they're no different.
   Half-blind man! Half open, half closed. What are you do-
   ing, clinging to fences and groping along walls? One cut,
   two pieces.
Adepts of all time have together been naming and describing.
   Twenty-eight (Patriarchs) in India, six in China, all the
   old teachers in the world, numerous as hemp and millet
   seeds—yet you have still left yourself out.
If you want to see the yellow-faced old fellow right now,
   Bah! The old barbarian! Blind fellow! He's right at your
   feet.
Each atom of every land lies halfway there.
   Where you stand you've already missed him. What more
   would you have me say? Will you ever see him, even in a
   dream?

COMMENTARY

"The Whole Elephant or the Whole Ox—as blinding cataracts, they're no different." A group of blind people groping over an elephant each speaks of a different aspect; this comes from the *Nirvana* scripture. A monk asked Yang Shan, "Master, when you saw someone come and ask about Ch'an or ask about the Way, you then drew a circle, and wrote the word 'ox' inside it; where does the meaning of this lie?" Yang Shan said, "This too is an idle matter: if you immediately can understand, it doesn't come from outside; if you cannot understand immediately, you certainly don't recognize it. Now I ask you, what have the aged adepts in various places pointed out in your body as your Buddha-nature? Do you consider it that which speaks, or is it that which is silent? Is it not that which neither speaks nor is silent? Or do you consider everything to be it, or do you consider that everything is not it? If you acknowledge that which speaks as it, you are like the blind man who has grabbed on to the elephant's tail. If you acknowledge that which is silent as it, you are like the blind man grabbing the elephant's ear. If you acknowledge that which neither speaks nor is silent as it, you are like the blind man grabbing the elephant's trunk. If you say everything is it, you are like the blind man grabbing the elephant's four legs. If you say none are it, you abandon the original elephant and fall into the view of emptiness. According to what these blind men perceive, they just attribute different names and descriptions to the elephant. If you want to do right, just avoid groping over the elephant: do not say perceptive awareness is it, yet do not say that is not it."

The Sixth Patriarch said, "Enlightenment basically has no tree; the clear mirror also has no stand. Fundamentally there is not a single thing; how is it possible to be defiled by any dust?" He also said, "The Way fundamentally has no shape or form; wisdom itself is the Way. To attain this understanding is called true transcendent wisdom." One with clear eyes sees the elephant and apprehends its entire body; the seeing of Buddha nature is also like this.

The "whole ox" appears in the *Chuang-tzu:* Pao Ting, in cutting up oxen, never saw the whole ox; he followed the internal patterns to cut them apart; letting his cleaver glide freely, he did not need to add any further effort. In the time it takes to raise your eyes, head and horn, hoof and flesh were separated of their own accord. He did so for nineteen years, and his cleaver was still as sharp as though it had newly come from the whetstone. This is called the "whole ox." Although he was so excellent, Hsueh Tou says that even if you can be like this, the whole elephant and the whole ox are no different from blinding cataracts in the eyes. "Adepts of all time together name and describe." Even adepts still grope inside without finding. From Kasyapa on down through the patriarchs and masters of India and China, the old teachers all over the world are just naming and describing.

Hsueh Tou directly says, "If you want to see the old yellow-face[c] right now, every atom of dust in every land lies halfway there." Usually we say that each atom is a Buddha-land, each leaf is a Shakyamuni. Even when all the atomic particles in the cosmos can be seen in one atom, you're still only halfway there; there is still another half of the way yonder. But tell me, where is he? Old Shakyamuni didn't even know himself; how would you have me explain?

TRANSLATORS' NOTES

a.   The open ground symbolizes the stage of Buddhahood; the white ox symbolizes the Dharmakaya, the body of reality, the ultimate and universal body of all Buddhas. In the *Saddharmapundarika* scripture, the white ox symbolizes the unique vehicle of Buddhahood. See also the appendix on Tung Shan's three falls in volume two.

b.   This passage occurs in the second volume of the *Surangama* scripture; we have translated according to the Sung dynasty commentary of Tzu Jui. This scripture, whose title means "Heroic Going," describes many psychological states and pitfalls of meditation; it was one of the favorite scriptures of Ch'an students, and numerous quotations from it are to be found in the sayings of Ch'an masters.

c.   "Yellow-face" refers to Shakyamuni Buddha, who as a Buddha represents all Buddhas and Buddhahood in general; the Buddha was said to have golden skin, hence the epithet "yellow face."

Ch'ang Ch'ing's Three Poisons

POINTER

Where there is Buddha, do not stay; if you keep staying there, your head will sprout horns. Where there is no Buddha, quickly run past; if you don't run past, weeds will grow ten feet high.

Even if you are pure and naked, bare and clean, without mental activity outside of things, without things outside of mental activity, you still have not escaped standing by a stump waiting for a rabbit.[a]

But tell me, without being like any of this, how would you act? To test, I cite this to see.

CASE

Ch'ang Ch'ing once said, "Rather say that saints have the three poisons,[1] but do not say that the Tathagata has two kinds of speech.[2] I do not say the Tathagata is speechless,[3] just that he doesn't have two kinds of speech."[4]

Pao Fu said, "What is Tathagata speech?"[5]

Ch'ing said, "How could a deaf man hear?"[6]

Pao Fu said, "I knew you were talking on the secondary level."[7]

Ch'ing said, "What is Tathagata speech?"[8]

Pao Fu said, "Go drink tea."[9]

NOTES

1. Scorched grain doesn't sprout.
2. He has already slandered old Shakyamuni.
3. He is still making a fool of himself; already he has seven openings and eight holes.
4. Useless maundering. What third or fourth kind will you talk about?

601

5. He gives a good thrust; what will you say?
6. He addresses a plea to the sky. It's burst forth in profusion.
7. How can you fool a clear-eyed man? He snaps his nostrils around. Why stop at only the second level?
8. A mistake; yet he's getting somewhere.
9. Understood. But do you comprehend? Stumbled past.

COMMENTARY

Ch'ang Ch'ing and Pao Fu, while in the community of Hsueh Feng, were always reminding and awakening each other, engaging in discussion. One day casually talking like this, (Ch'ang Ch'ing) said, "Rather say that saints have the three poisons than say that the Tathagata has two kinds of speech." The Sanskrit word for saint, arhat, means killer of thieves;[b] by their virtue and accomplishment they illustrate their name; they cut off the nine times nine, or eighty-one kinds of passion, all their leaks are already dried up,[c] and their pure conduct is already established—this is the state of sainthood, where there is nothing more to learn. The three poisons are greed, hatred, and folly, the fundamental passions. If they have themselves completely cut off the eighty-one kinds (of passion), how much more so the three poisons! Ch'ang Ch'ing said, "Rather say that saints have the three poisons, but don't say that the Tathagata has two kinds of speech." His general idea was that he wanted to show that the Tathagata does not say anything untrue. In the Lotus of Truth scripture it says, "Only this one thing is true;[d] any second besides is not real." It also says, "There is only one vehicle of truth; there is no second or third." The World Honored One, in over three hundred assemblies, observed potentiality to set down his teachings, giving medicine in accordance with the disease: in ten thousand kinds and a thousand varieties of explanations of the Dharma, ultimately there are no two kinds of speech. His idea having gotten this far, how can you people see? The Buddha widely taught the Dharma with One Voice; this I don't deny—but Ch'ang Ch'ing actually has never seen the Tathagata's speech even in a dream. Why? It's just like a man talking about food—after all that can't satisfy his hunger. Pao Fu saw him talking about the doctrine on level ground, so he asked, "What is Tathagata speech?" Ch'ing said, "How can a deaf man hear it?" This fellow (Pao Fu) knew that (Ch'ang Ch'ing) had been making his living in a ghost cave for some time; Pao Fu said, "I knew you were speaking on the secondary level." And after all (Ch'ang Ch'ing) lived up to these words; he asked back, "Elder brother, what is Tathagata speech?" Fu said, "Go drink tea." (Ch'ang Ch'ing) had his spear snatched away by someone else; Ch'ang Ch'ing, supposedly so great, lost his money and incurred punishment.

Now I ask everyone, how many (kinds of) Tathagata speech are there? You should know that only when you can see in this way, then you will see the defeat of these two fellows. If you examine thoroughly, everyone should be beaten. I'll let out a pathway, to let others comprehend. Some say that Pao Fu spoke correctly, and that Ch'ang Ch'ing spoke incorrectly; they just follow words to produce interpretations, so they say there is gain and loss. They are far from knowing that the Ancients were like stone struck sparks, like flashing lightning. People nowadays do not go to the Ancients' turning point to look; they just go running to the phrases and say, "Ch'ang Ch'ing didn't immediately act; therefore he fell into the secondary lvel. Pao Fu's saying 'Go drink tea' is the primary level." If you only look at it in this way, even by the time Maitreya Buddha comes down to be born here, you still won't see the Ancients' meaning. If you are an adept, you will never entertain such a view; leaping out of this nest of cliché, you'll have your own road upward.

If you say, "What is wrong with 'How could a deaf man hear?'? What is right about 'Go drink tea'?" Then you are even further from it. For this reason it is said, "He studies the living phrase, he doesn't study the dead phrase." This story is the same as the story of "It is all over the body; it is all through the body"ᵉ—there is nowhere you can judge and compare right or wrong. It is necessary for you to be clean and naked right where you stand; only then will you see where the Ancients met. My late teacher Wu Tsu said, "It is like coming to grips on the front line." It requires a discerning eye and a familiar hand. In this public case, if you see it with the true eye, where there is neither gain nor loss, it distinguishes gain and loss; where there is no near or far, it distinguishes near and far. Ch'ang Ch'ing still should have bowed to Pao Fu to be proper. Why?

Because (Pao Fu) used this little bit of skill well, like thunder rolling or a comet flying. But Pao Fu couldn't help but produce tooth upon tooth, nail upon nail.

VERSE

Primary, secondary:
> In my royal storehouse, there are no such things. The standard for past and present. What are you doing, following the false and pursuing the bad?

A reclining dragon does not look to still water—
> Only one on the same road would know.

Where he is not, there is the moon; the waves settle:
> Over the four seas the solitary boat goes by itself. It is useless to trouble to figure it out. What bowl are you looking for?

Where he is, waves arise without wind.
> He threatens people ferociously; do you feel your hair standing on end in a chill? Striking, I say, "He's come!"

O Ch'an traveller Leng! Ch'an traveller Leng!
> He takes in a thief, who ransacks his house. Do not appear in a bustling marketplace. He lost his money and incurred punishment.

In the third month, at the Gate of Yü, you've got a failing mark.
> Not one in ten thousand can withdraw himself and defer to others. He can only suck in his breath and swallow his voice.

COMMENTARY

"Primary, secondary." If people only theoretically understand primary and secondary, this indeed is making a living in dead water. This active skill, if you only understand it in terms of first or second, you will still be unable to get hold of it. Hsueh Tou says, "A reclining dragon does not look to still water." In dead water, how can there be a dragon hidden? If it is "primary and secondary," this indeed is making a livelihood in dead stagnant water. There must be huge swells wide and vast, white waves flooding the sky; only there can a dragon be concealed. It is just like was said before; "A limpid pond does not admit the blue dragon's coils." Have you not heard it said, "Stagnant water does not contain a dragon." And it is said, "A reclining dragon is always wary of the clarity of the blue pond." That is why (Hsueh Tou) says that where there is no dragon, there is the moon, the waves settle—the wind is calm, the waves grow still. Where there is a dragon, waves rise without wind; much like Pao Fu's saying "Go drink tea"—this indeed is rousing waves without wind. Hsueh Tou at this point cleans up emotional interpretations for you, and has completed the verse. He has extra rhymes, so he makes the pattern complete; as before he sets a single eye on the content, and again is undeniably outstanding. He says, "O Ch'an traveller Leng! Ch'an traveller Leng!ᶠ In the third month at the Gate of Yü, you get a failing mark."ᵍ Although Ch'ang Ch'ing was a dragon who had passed through the Dragon Gate, yet he got a tap right on the head from Pao Fu.

TRANSLATORS' NOTES

a. A fool once saw a rabbit run into a stump and die; he waited by the stump, hoping it would "catch" another rabbit for him. See case 10.
b. *Arhat* also means "worthy"; that is, worthy of offerings.
c. "Leaks" are passions, attachments, defilements; the flow of energy into habitual patterns of clinging, into emotional involvement with the world, draining people of their will and making them slaves of passion. The four knowledges of sainthood—*arhat*ship—are that one's leaks are dried up—that is, one is free from affectation and affliction, that pure conduct has been established, that one has done what was to be done, and that one is freed from further existence in the profane state.
d. The main idea of this scripture is that all sentient beings will eventually realize Buddhahood, perfect enlightenment; "this one thing" is the knowledge and vision of Buddhas—the one vehicle is the vehicle of Buddhahood, within which the vehicles of discipleship, leading to sainthood, and of self-enlightenment through

understanding the conditions of confusion and suffering, are shown to be provisional teachings designed for beings of lesser capacity and inspiration who are temporarily unable to bear the burdens of bodhisattvahood on the way to the unexcelled perfect enlightenment of all Buddhas.

e. See case 89.

f. Ch'ang Ch'ing's personal initiatory name was Hui Leng; it was standard practice to refer to someone by the second syllable of the name.

g. According to legend, fish who can leap past the Dragon Gate (which is called the Gate of Yü because it was built under the direction of the great king Yü in the latter part of the third millennium B.C. during the time of a great flood in northern China) turn into dragons and soar off into the clouds. In Chinese literary convention this is used to symbolize the civil service examinations; those who pass and are eligible for official posts are likened to the fish who have become dragons. In Ch'an this is used to symbolize the attainment of enlightenment. This first appears in the seventh case, q.v., and recurs several times in this book.

Chao Chou's Three Turning Words

CASE

Chao Chou expressed three turning words to his community.[1] ("A gold Buddha does not pass through a furnace; a wood Buddha does not pass through fire; a mud Buddha does not pass through water.")

NOTES

1. What did he say? The three parts are not the same.

COMMENTARY

After Chao Chou had spoken these three turning words, in the end he said, "The real Buddha sits within." This phrase is exceedingly indulgent. That man of old set forth a single eye, extended his hand to guide people; briefly making use of these words to convey the message, he wanted to help others. If you one-sidedly bring up the true imperative in its entirety, there would be weeds ten feet deep in front of the teaching hall. Hsueh Tou dislikes the indulgence of that final phrase, so he omits it and just versifies three phrases. If a mud Buddha passes through water it will dissolve; if a gold Buddha passes through a furnace it will melt; if a wood Buddha passes through fire it will burn up. What is difficult to understand about this? Hsueh Tou's hundred examples of eulogizing the Ancients are complicated with judgments and comparisons; only these three verses directly contain the breath of a patchrobed monk. However, these verses are nevertheless difficult to understand. If you can pass through these three verses, I'll allow as you have finished studying.

VERSE (1)

A mud Buddha does not pass through water:
   He's soaked it till the nose decomposes. Without wind he
   raises waves.

Spiritual Light illumines heaven and earth;
   Seeing a rabbit, he releases a hawk. What has it got to do
   with others?

Standing in the snow, if he didn't rest,
   When one person transmits a falsehood, ten thousand
   people transmit it as truth. He adds error to error. Who
   has ever seen you?

Who would not carve an imitation?
   Upon entering a temple, you see its nameplate. Running
   up and running down twenty-four hours a day—what is
   it? You are it.

COMMENTARY

"A mud Buddha does not pass through water: Spiritual Light
illumines heaven and earth." This one phrase clearly com-
pletes the verse: but tell me, why does he mention Shen Kuang
("Spiritual Light")? When the Second Patriarch was first born, a
spiritual light illumined the room, extending into the sky. Also
one night a spirit appeared and said to the Second Patriarch,
"Why remain here long? The time for you to attain the Way
has arrived: you should go South." Because of his association
with spirits, the Second Patriarch was eventually named Shen
Kuang (which means "Spiritual Light"). He lived for a long
time in the Yi-Lo area (Loyang), and widely studied many
books. He always lamented, "The teachings of Confucius and
Lao Tzu only transmit customary norms. Recently I have heard
that the great teacher Bodhidharma is dwelling at Shao Lin." So
he went there, visiting and knocking day and night; but
Bodhidharma sat still, and gave no instruction. Kuang thought
to himself, "When people of ancient times sought the Way,
they broke their bones and took out the marrow, shed their
blood to appease hunger, spread their hair to cover mud, threw
themselves off cliffs to feed tigers. Even of old they were like
this; what about me?"

That year on the night of the ninth of December there was a great snow. The Second Patriarch stood by the wall; by dawn the snow had piled up past his knees. Bodhidharma took pity on him and said, "You, standing in the snow there; what do you seek?" The Second Patriarch sighed sadly and said, "I only beg your compassion, to open up the gate of ambrosia, and save all creatures." Bodhidharma said, "The wondrous path of all the Buddhas requires zealous work over vast aeons, practicing that which is difficult to practice, enduring the unendurable; with little virtue and petty knowledge, a shallow heart and arrogant mind, how can you hope to seek the true vehicle? There is no way." The Second Patriarch, hearing this admonition, was even more earnest towards the Path; he secretly took a sharp knife and cut off his own left forearm, and placed it before Bodhidharma. Bodhidharma knew he was a vessel of Dharma, so he asked him, "You stand in the snow and cut off your arm; what for?" The Second Patriarch said, "My mind is not yet at ease. Please, Master, ease my mind." Bodhidharma said, "Bring forth your mind, and I will ease it for you." The Second Patriarch said, "When I search for my mind, ultimately I can't find it." Bodhidharma said, "I have put your mind at ease for you." Afterwards Bodhidharma changed (Shen Kuang's) name to Hui K'e. Later (Hui K'e) taught the Third Patriarch, Great Master Seng Ts'an.

So Hsueh Tou says, "Standing in the snow, if he didn't rest, who would not carve an imitation?" Slavishly fawning deceitful people would all imitate him, at once becoming mere contrived false imitations: these are the obsequious phoney followers. Hsueh Tou is eulogizing "A mud Buddha does not pass through water"—why then does he bring up this story? He had reached the absence of anything at all in his mind; clean and naked, only thus could he versify like this.

Wu Tsu always used to have people look at these three verses. Have you not seen how Master Shou Ch'u of Tung Shan had a verse which he showed his community, saying,

Atop Mount Wu T'ai, clouds are steaming rice;
In front of the Ancient Buddha Hall, a dog is pissing
  skyward.
Frying cakes atop the flagpole,
Three monkeys pitch pennies in the night.

And Master Tu Shun said,

> When oxen in Huai province eat grain,
> The bellies of horses in Yi province are distended;
> Looking for a doctor all over the world
> To cauterize a pig's left arm.

And Mahasattva Fu said,

> Empty handed, holding a hoe,
> Walking, riding a water buffalo,
> A man is crossing over a bridge;
> The bridge, not the water, flows.

It is also said,

> If the capacity of a stone man were like you,
> He too could sing folk songs;
> If you were like a stone man,
> You too could join in the opera.

If you can understand these words, then you will understand that verse of Hsueh Tou's.

VERSE (2)

A gold Buddha does not pass through a furnace;
  He burns off the eyebrows. "In the heavens and on earth, I alone am the Honored One."
Someone comes calling on Tzu Hu;
  He goes this way too? I only fear he'll lose his life.
On the sign, several words—
  An illiterate would have no way of understanding even if it were about a cat. No patchrobed monk in the world can get his teeth in.
Where is there no pure wind?
  You go this way too? Above the head it is vast and boundless; below the feet, vast and boundless. I also say, "It's arrived."

COMMENTARY

"A gold Buddha does not pass through a furnace; / A man comes calling on Tzu Hu." This one phrase has also completed

the verse. Why does he bring up "someone calling on Tzu Hu"?
Only with the forge and bellows of a Master is it possible.
Master Tzu Hu set up a sign on his outside gate; on the sign
were words saying, "Tzu Hu has a dog: above, he takes people's
heads; in the middle, he takes people's loins; below, he takes
people's legs. If you stop to talk to him, you'll lose your body
and life." Whenever he saw a newcomer, he would immediately shout and say, "Watch out for the dog!" As soon as
the monk turned his head, Tzu Hu would immediately return
to the abbot's room. But tell me, why could he not bite Chao
Chou? Tzu Hu also once late at night shouted in the lavatory,
"Catch the thief! Catch the thief!" In the dark he ran into a
monk; he grabbed him by the chest and held him, saying,
"Caught him! Caught him!" The monk said, "Master, it's not
me." Hu said, "It is, but you just won't own up to it." If you can
understand this story, then you may chew everyone to death;
everywhere the pure wind will be chill and severe. If not, you
will certainly not be able to do anything about "the several
words on the sign." If you want to see him, just pass through
completely and then you will see what the verse is saying.

VERSE (3)

A wood Buddha does not pass through fire;
  Burned up! Only I can know.
I always think of the Oven Breaker—
  Going east, going west, what is wrong? A leper drags a
  companion along.
The staff suddenly strikes,
  It is in my hands. I still don't need it. Who doesn't have it
  in his hands?
And then one realizes he'd turned away from his self.
  Just like you. If you can't find it out, what use is it? Alas!
  Alas! After thirty years you'll finally get it. It is better to
  be sunk forever than to see the liberation of the saints. If
  you can seize it here, you'll still not avoid turning away.
  How to be able not to turn away? The staff is still in
  another's hands.

COMMENTARY

"A wood Buddha does not pass through fire; / I always think of the Oven Breaker." This one phrase also has completed the verse. Hsueh Tou, because of this "wood Buddha does not pass through fire," always thinks of the Oven Breaker. The "Oven Breaker Monk" of Mount Sung was not known by any surname; his speech and behavior were unfathomable. He dwelt in seclusion on Mount Sung. One day, leading a group of followers, he went among the mountain aborigines: they had a shrine which was most sacred; in its hall was placed only an oven. People from far and near sacrificed to it unceasingly; they had immolated very many living creatures. The Master entered the shrine and tapped the oven three times with his staff. He said, "What humbug! You were originally made of brick and mud compounded; where does the spirit come from, whence does the sanctity originate, that you burn living creatures to death like this?" And again he hit it three times. The oven then toppled over, broke and collapsed of itself. Momentarily there was a man in a blue robe and tall hat suddenly standing in front of the Master; bowing, he said, "I am the god of the oven; for a long time I have been subject to retribution for actions, but today, hearing the Master explain the truth of non-origination, I am already freed from this place, and living in heaven. I have come especially to offer thanks." The Master said, "It is your fundamentally inherent nature, not my forced saying so." The god again bowed, and disappeared. An attendant said, "I and others have been around the Master for a long time, but have never received instruction. What shortcut did the oven god find, that he was immediately born in heaven?" The Master said, "I just said to him, 'You were originally made of brick and mud put together; where does the spirit come from, whence does the sanctity emerge?'" The attendant had no reply. The Master said, "Do you understand?" The monk said, "I do not understand." The Master said, "Bow!" The monk bowed; the Master said, "Broken! Collapsed!" The attendant was suddenly greatly enlightened.

Later a certain monk reported this to National Teacher Hui An. The Teacher sighed in admiration and said, "This lad has comprehended thoroughly things and self as one suchness."

The oven god understood this principle, therefore he was thus: that monk was a body composed of five heaps; (the Master) also said, "Broken! Collapsed!" Both opened to enlightenment, but tell me, are the four elements and five heaps the same as or different from brick and tiles, mud and earth? Since it is so, why does Hsueh Tou say, "The staff suddenly strikes; (the oven god) then realizes he had turned away from his self"? Why does one become turned away? It is just a matter of not yet having found the staff.

And tell me, as Hsueh Tou eulogizes "a wood Buddha does not pass through fire," why does he cite the public case of the oven breaking and collapsing? I will explain it directly for you; his intention is just to cut off feelings and ideas of gain and loss; once cleaned and naked, you will naturally see his kindness.

The Diamond Cutter Scripture's Scornful Revilement

POINTER

If you take up one and let two go, you are not yet an adept; even to understand three corners when one is raised still goes against the fundamental essence. Even if you get heaven and earth to change instantly, without rejoinder from the four quarters, thunder rolling and lightning flying, clouds moving and rain rushing, overturning lakes and toppling cliffs, like a pitcher pouring, like a bowl emptying, you have still not raised up a half. Is there anyone who can turn the polar star, who can shift the axis of the earth? To test, I cite this to see.

CASE

The Diamond Cutter scripture says, "If one is scornfully reviled by others,[1] this person has done wicked acts in previous ages[2] which should bring him down into evil ways,[3] but because of the scorn and vilification by others in the present age,[4] the wicked action of former ages[5] is thereby extinguished."[6]

NOTES

1. It lets out a pathway. And what is wrong with that?
2. Assloads, horseloads.
3. He's already fallen.
4. Paying off the roots has effects that extend to the branches. He can only accept it with forbearance.
5. Where can you seek for it? Planting grain will not produce beans.
6. This is adding another layer of frost upon snow. It's like boiling water melting ice.

COMMENTARY

In the Diamond Cutter scripture[a] it says, "If one is scorned and vilified by other people, the fact is that this person has done evil actions in former ages which should bring him down into evil ways; but because of the scornful revilement of people in this age, the wicked action of former ages is thereby extinguished." According to the ordinary way of interpretation, this is the constant theme throughout the scripture. Hsueh Tou brings it up and versifies this meaning; he wants to break up the scholastic schools' livelihood in the ghost caves. Prince Chao Ming[b] singled out this part and considered it able to clear away obstruction by former deeds.

The general idea of the scripture talks about the efficacy of this scripture: someone like this in former times created hellish deeds, but because of the strength of its good power, he has not yet suffered. Because of scorn and vilification by people in the present age, the wicked action of former ages is thereby extinguished. This scripture therefore can extinguish the wicked deeds of innumerable aeons, changing the grave to become light, changing the light to being inconsequential, and furthermore bringing the attainment of enlightenment, the fruit of Buddhahood.

According to the scholastic schools, turning[c] this twenty-odd page scripture is itself called "upholding the scripture," but what connection is there? Some say that the scripture itself has spiritual power. If so, take a volume and lay it in an uncluttered place; see if there is any effect or not. Fa Yen said, "Realizing Buddhahood is called 'upholding this scripture.'" In the scripture it says, "All the Buddhas and the teaching of complete perfect awakening of all the Buddhas, all comes forth from this scripture." But tell me, what do you call "this scripture"? Is it not that with yellow scrolls on red rollers? Don't mistakenly stick by the zero point of the scale.

The Diamond is likened to the body of truth: because it is hard and solid, things cannot break it; because of its sharp cutting function, it can break anything. Apply it to a mountain, and the mountain crumbles; apply it to the sea, and the sea dries up. The name is expressed in metaphor, and so is its activity.

This wisdom is of three kinds: the first is the wisdom of the character of reality, the second is observant illumination wisdom, and the third is verbal wisdom. The wisdom of the character of reality is true knowledge: it is the one great matter where each of you stands, shining across past and present, far beyond knowledge and opinion; it is that which is clean and naked, bare and untrammelled. Observant illumination wisdom is the real world; it is that which emits light and moves the earth twenty-four hours a day, hearing sound and seeing form. Verbal wisdom is the language which can express it; that is, the present speaker and hearer. But tell me, is this wisdom or is it not wisdom? An Ancient said, "Everyone has a volume of scripture." It has also been said, "My hand does not hold a scripture scroll, but I am always turning such a scripture."

If you depend on this scripture's spiritual efficacy, why stop at just making the serious trifling, and making the trifling totally inconsequential? Even if you could match the ability of the sages, that would still not be anything special.

Have you not seen how Layman P'ang, listening to an exposition of the Diamond Cutter scripture, asked the lecturer, "A layman dares to have a small question; is that all right?" The lecturer said, "If you have a doubt, please ask." The layman said, "'There is no sign of self, no sign of others'—since there is no sign of self or others, who would you have lecture, who would you have listen?" The lecturer had no reply; instead he said, "I just interpret the meaning according to the letter; I do not know the meaning of this." The layman then said in verse,

> No self and no others; how could there be near or
>   far?
> I urge you to stop going through lectures;
> How could that be compared to seeking the real
>   directly?
> The nature of adamantine wisdom is devoid of a
>   single particle of dust;
> 'I have heard' through 'I faithfully accept'
> Are all just artificial names.

This verse is most excellent; it has clearly explained all at once.

Kuei Feng picked out a four line stanza, saying, "Whatever is seen, all is empty falsehood; if you see that various forms are not forms, then you see the Tathagata." The meaning of this four line stanza is exactly the same as "Realizing Buddhahood is called 'upholding this scripture.'"

It is also said (in the scripture), "If one sees me by means of form, if he seeks me by means of sound, this person is traversing a false path; he cannot see the Tathagata." This too is a four line stanza; we just take from among them those whose meaning is complete. A monk asked Hui T'ang, "What is the four line stanza?" Hui T'ang said, "Your talk is degenerate, yet you don't even realize it."

Hsueh Tou points out what is in this scripture. If there is someone who can uphold this scripture, then this is the scenery of everyone's original ground, the original face: but if you act according to the Patriarchs' imperative, the scenery of the original ground, the original face, would still be cut into three pieces; the twelve-part teachings of the Buddhas of the three times wouldn't be worth a pinch. At this point, even if you had the ten thousand varieties of skill, you still couldn't handle them. Nowadays people only revolve scriptures and do not know what the principle is at all. They merely say, "In one day, I have revolved so many." They only recognize the yellow scrolls on red rollers, perusing the lines and counting the inkmarks. They are far from realizing that it all arises from their own original minds, that this is only a bit of a turning point.

Master Ta Chu said, "Pile up several cases of scriptures in an empty room, and see if they emit light." It's just your own mind, inspired in a single moment of thought, that is the virtue. Why? Myriad things all come forth from one's own mind. One moment of thought is aware; once aware, it pervades; having pervaded, it transforms. An Ancient said, "The green bamboos are all true thusness; the lush yellow flowers are all wisdom." If you can see all the way through, then this is true thusness; but if you have not yet seen, tell me, what do you call true thusness? The Flower Garland scripture says, "If a person wants to know all the Buddhas of past, present, and future, he should observe that the nature of the cosmos is all just the fabrication of mind." If you can discern, then in whatever situations or circumstances you meet, you'll be the master and the source. If you cannot yet get it clear, then humbly listen to the verdict: Hsueh Tou puts forth an eye and versifies the main theme, wishing to clarify the scripture's spiritual efficacy.

VERSE

The clear jewel is in my palm;
  Above, it goes through the sky; below, it penetrates the
  Yellow Springs (Hades). What is he saying? Impenetrable
  on four sides, crystal clear on eight faces.

Whoever has accomplishment will be rewarded with it.
  Quite clear; it would go along with him. If there were no
  accomplishment, how would you reward it?

When neither foreigner nor native comes
  Inside and outside are void of happenings. Still this
  amounts to something.

It has utterly no abilities.
  More and more irrelevant. Where would you look for it?
  Come break the lacquer bucket and I'll meet with you.

Since it has no abilities,
  Stop, rest, Who is speaking this way?

The Evil One loses the way.
  Outsiders and the king of demons cannot find any tracks.

Gautama, Gautama!
  Even the Buddha-eye cannot see in. Bah!

Do you know me or not?
  Bah!

(Hsueh Tou also said,) "Completely exposed!"
  Each blow of the staff leaves a welt. It was already so
  before it was said.

COMMENTARY

"The clear jewel is in my palm; to whoever has accomplishment, I'll reward it." If there is someone who can uphold this
scripture with actual effect, then he is rewarded with the jewel.
When he gets this jewel, he will naturally know how to use it:
when a foreigner comes, a foreigner is reflected; when a native
comes, a native is reflected—myriad forms and appearances,
vertically and horizontally, are clearly reflected. This is having
actual accomplishment. These two lines have finished versifying the public case.

"When neither foreigner nor native comes, it is utterly without abilities." (Here) Hsueh Tou turns your nose around. When foreigners or natives appear, then he has you reflect them; if neither foreigner nor native comes, then what? When he gets here, even the Buddha's eye cannot see in. But tell me, is this accomplishment, or is it wicked action? Is he a foreigner? Is he a native? He's just like the antelope with his horns hung up: do not say there is any sound or trace of him—there is not even a breath; where could you go to search for him? He has gotten to where there is no road on which to have the gods offer flowers, no gate through which demons and outsiders might secretly spy. That is why the Master of Tung Shan dwelt all his life in the temple, but the earth spirit couldn't find any trace of him. One day someone spilled rice flour in the kitchen; Tung Shan aroused his mind and said, "How can you treat the communal supplies with such contempt?" So the earth spirit finally got to see him; thereupon he bowed.

Hsueh Tou says, "Since there are no abilities;" if you reach the point where there is no ability, you will make even the Evil One, the king of demons, lose the way. The World Honored One regarded all sentient beings as his children: if there is one person who rouses his mind to practice, the palace of the Evil One would tremble and split because of this, and the demons would come to torment and confuse the practitioner. Hsueh Tou says that even if the Evil One comes like this, still one must make him lose his way and have no avenue of approach.

Hsueh Tou goes on to point to himself and say, "Gautama, Gautama! / Do you know me or not?" Do not even speak of demons; even should the Buddha come, would he know me or not? Even old Shakyamuni himself couldn't see him; where will you people search for him? He also said, "Completely exposed." But tell me, is this Hsueh Tou exposing Gautama, or is it Gautama exposing Hsueh Tou? Those who have eyes, try to see for sure.

TRANSLATORS' NOTES

a.   This is the *(Prajnaparamita) Vajracchedika sutra.* This was one of the most popular scriptures in China, and studied by most Ch'an students. The Sixth Patriarch of Ch'an, Hui Neng, was first enlightened when he chanced to hear a passage of this scripture being recited in a marketplace where he was selling wood; Hung Jen, the Fifth Patriarch, was said to have used it in his teaching. See also the fourth case, volume one.

b. Prince Chao Ming was the son of the Emperor Wu of Liang; he was an outstanding scholar, fond of Buddhist studies like his famous father. See the first case, in volume one.

c. "Turning" or "revolving" means recitation; usually, in the case of long scriptures, it means reciting snatches of the scripture while skipping rapidly through. Mahasattva Fu invented a revolving case for the canon, so that all of the scriptures could be "turned" at once by this device; usually memorized passages of scripture are recited while turning the whole canon.

T'ien P'ing's Travels on Foot

POINTER^a

Collecting the causes, producing the result, completing the beginning, completing the end. Face to face, there is nothing hidden, but fundamentally I have never explained. If there is suddenly someone who comes forth and says, "All summer we've been asking for instruction; why have you never explained?"—Wait till you've awakened, then I'll tell you.

Tell me, do you think that this is avoidance of direct confrontation, or do you think it has some other merit? To test, I cite this to see.

CASE

When the Master of T'ien P'ing was travelling on foot, he called on Hsi Yuan. He always would say, "Do not say you understand the Buddhist Teaching; I cannot find a single man who can quote a saying."[1]

One day Hsi Yuan saw him from a distance and called him by name: "Ts'ung Yi!"[2]

P'ing raised his head:[3] Hsi Yuan said, "Wrong!"[4] P'ing went two or three steps;[5] Hsi Yuan again said, "Wrong!"[6] P'ing approached;[7] Hsi Huan said, "These two wrongs just now: were they my wrongs or your wrongs?"[8]

P'ing said, "My wrongs."[9]

Hsi Yuan said, "Wrong!"[10] P'ing gave up.[11] Hsi Yuan said, "Stay here for the summer and wait for me to discuss these two wrongs with you."[12]

But P'ing immediately went away.[13] Later, when he was dwelling in a temple, he said to his community,[14] "When I was first travelling on foot, I was blown by the wind of events to Elder Ssu Ming's place: twice in a row he said 'Wrong!' and tried to keep me there over the summer to wait for him to deal with me. I did not say it was wrong then; when I set out for the South, I already knew that it was wrong."[15]

NOTES

1. He's let slip quite a bit. This fellow is right, but nevertheless he's like the sacred tortoise dragging his tail.
2. The hook is set.
3. Got him! A double case.
4. Still he must have been tempered in a furnace before being able. He splits his guts and wounds his heart. When the seal of the three essentials is lifted, the red spot is narrow; before any attempt to discuss it, host and guest are distinguished.
5. Already he's fallen halfway behind. This fellow is washing a clod of dirt in the mud.
6. Splits his guts and wounds his heart. Everyone calls this a double case, but they do not know it is like putting water in water, like exchanging gold for gold.
7. As before, he doesn't know where to rest. More and more he gropes without finding.
8. The first arrows were still light; this last arrow goes deep.
9. He mistakes a saddle ridge for his father's lower jaw.[b] As for such patchrobed monks as this one, even if you killed a thousand or ten thousand of them, what crime would it be?
10. He adds frost to snow.
11. He mistakenly goes by the zero point of the scale. After all he doesn't know where to rest. I knew his nostrils were in someone else's hand.
12. Hsi Yuan's spine is usually hard as iron; why did he not immediately drive (T'ien P'ing) away?
13. He still resembles a patchrobed monk; he resembles one, but isn't really.
14. A poor man thinks of his old debts. Still it is necessary to check.
15. What can he do about the two wrongs? A thousand "wrongs," ten thousand "wrongs"; nonetheless it's all irrelevant. All the more he shows his senility and saddens others.

COMMENTARY

Master Ts'ung Yi of T'ien P'ing, travelling on foot, went to see Hsi Yuan. Ssu Ming of Hsi Yuan had first called on Ta Hsueh, and later succeeded to the former Pao Shou. One day he asked, "How is it after trampling down the Temporary Citadel of

nirvana?" Shou said, "A sharp sword does not cut a dead man."
Ming said, "Cut!" Shou thereupon hit him. Ssu Ming said
"Cut!" ten times, and Shou hit him ten times and said, "What
is this fellow's big hurry to take this dead corpse and submit it
to another's painful staff?" Finally he shouted and drove Ssu
Ming out. At that time there was a monk who asked Pao Shou,
"That monk who just asked a question is quite reasonable,
Master; deal with him appropriately." Pao Shou hit him too,
driving out this monk. But tell me, when Pao Shou also drove
out this monk, can you say it was just because he was speaking
of right and wrong, or is there another reason? What was his
idea? Later they both succeeded to Pao Shou.

Ssu Ming one day went to see Nan Yuan. Yuan asked him,
"Where do you come from?" Ming said, "From Hsu Chou."
Yuan said, "What did you bring?" Ming said, "I brought a razor
from Kiangsi; I offer it to you." Yuan said, "Since you come
from Hsu Chou, how is it that you have a razor from Kiangsi?"
Ming took Yuan's hand and pinched it once. Yuan said, "Attendant! Take him away!" Ssu Ming gave a whisk of his sleeve
and left. Yuan said, "O wow!"

T'ien P'ing had once called on the Master of Chin Shan.
Because he had gone to various places and attained this
turnip-Ch'an and put it in his belly, everywhere he went he
scornfully opened his big mouth and said, "I understand Ch'an,
I understand the Way." He always said, "Do not say you understand the Buddhist Teaching; I cannot find even a single man
who can quote a saying." His stinking breath affected others,
and he only indulged in scorn and contempt.

Before the Buddha had appeared in the world, before the
Patriarch had come from the West, before there were questions
and answers, before there were public cases, was there any
Ch'an Way? The Ancients could not avoid imparting teachings
according to potentialities; people later called them "public
cases." As the World Honored One raised a flower, Kasyapa
smiled; later on, Ananda asked Kasyapa, "The World Honored
One handed on his golden-sleeved robe; what special teaching
did he transmit to you besides?" Kasyapa said, "Ananda!"
Ananda responded; Kasyapa said, "Take down the flagpole in
front of the monastery gate." But before the flower was raised,
before Ananda had asked, where do you find any public cases?
You just accept the winter melon seals of various places, and

once the seal is set, you then immediately say, "I understand
the marvel of the Buddhist Teaching! Don't let anyone know!"

T'ien P'ing was just like this: when Hsi Yuan called him to
come and then said, "Wrong!" twice in a row, right away he
was confused and bewildered, unable to give any explanations;
he "neither got to the village nor reached the shop." Some say
that to speak of the meaning of the coming from the West is
already wrong; they are far from knowing what these two
wrongs of Hsi Yuan ultimately come down to. You people tell
me, what do they come down to? This is why it is said, "He
studies the living word, not the dead word." When T'ien P'ing
raised his head, he had already fallen into two and three. Hsi
Yuan said, "Wrong." But (T'ien P'ing) did not grasp his
straightforward action, but just said, "I have a bellyful of
Ch'an," and didn't pay any attention to him, and went two or
three steps. Hsi Yuan again said, "Wrong!" But T'ien P'ing was
as muddled as before, and approached Hsi Yuan. Yuan said,
"The two wrongs just now; were they my wrongs or your
wrongs?" T'ien P'ing said, "My wrongs." Fortunately, there is
no connection. Already he had fallen into seventh and eighth
place. Hsi Yuan said, "Just stay here for the summer and wait
for me to discuss these two wrongs with you." T'ien P'ing
immediately went away. He seemed to be right, but wasn't
really. Then again, I don't say he wasn't right; it's just that he
couldn't catch up. Nevertheless, he still had something of the
air of a patchrobed monk.

When T'ien P'ing later was dwelling in a temple, he said to
his community, "When I was first travelling on foot, I was
blown by the wind of events to Master Ssu Ming's place. Twice
he said 'Wrong!' and tried to have me pass the summer there to
wait for him to deliberate with me. I did not say it was wrong
then; when I set out for the South, I already knew that it was
wrong." This old fellow has said quite a bit; it's just that he's
fallen into seventh and eighth place, shaking his head thinking,
out of touch. When people these days hear him saying, "When I
set out for the South, I already knew that it was wrong," they
immediately go figuring it out and say, "Before even going on
foot travels, there is naturally not so much Buddhism or Ch'an;
and when you go foot travelling, you are completely fooled by
people everywhere. Even before foot travels, you can't call
earth sky or call mountains rivers; fortunately there is nothing

to be concerned about at all." If you all entertain such common vulgar views, why not buy a bandanna to wear and pass your time in the boss's house? What is the use? Buddha's teaching is not this principle. If you discuss this matter, how could there be so many complications? If you say, "I understand, others do not understand," carrying a bundle of Ch'an around the country, when you are tried out by clear-eyed people, you won't be able to use it at all. Hsueh Tou versifies in exactly this way:

VERSE

Followers of the Ch'an house
    The lacquer buckets all have their crimes listed on the same indictment.
Like to be scornful:
    Still there are some (who are otherwise). Those who scold Buddhas and revile Patriarchs are as plentiful as hemp and millet.
Having studied till their bellies are full, they cannot put it to use.
    It would be best to have use. A square peg does not fit in a round hole. You are a fellow student of theirs.
How lamentable, laughable old T'ien P'ing;
    No patchrobed monk in the world can leap out. He doesn't fear that bystanders may frown. Still he's gotten people to foolishly fret.
After all he says at the outset it was regrettable to go travel on foot.
    He was already wrong before he had gone travelling. Wearing out sandals, what is the use? He blots it out with one brush stroke.
Wrong, wrong!
    What is this? Hsueh Tou has already wrongly named it.
Hsi Yuan's pure wind suddenly melts him.
    Where is Hsi Yuan? What is it like? Do not speak only of Hsi Yuan; even the Buddhas of past, present, and future and the old masters everywhere also must fall back three thousand miles. If you can understand here, you may travel freely anywhere.

(Hsueh Tou) also said, "Suppose there is suddenly a patchrobed monk who comes out and says, 'Wrong';[1] how does Hsueh Tou's wrong compare to T'ien P'ing's wrong?"[2]

NOTES TO PROSE

1. The crimes are listed on the same indictment. He's still gotten somewhere.
2. Hsi Yuan again appears in the world. He settles the case according to the facts. Totally irrelevant. But tell me, after all, how is it? Striking, I say "Wrong!"

COMMENTARY

"Followers of the Ch'an house like to be scornful; having studied till their bellies are full, they can't put it to use." This fellow understood, as far as understanding goes; it's just that he couldn't use it. He always gazed at the cloudy sky and said he understood so much Ch'an; but when he was heated a little in the fireplace, it turned out that he couldn't use it at all. My late Master Wu Tsu said, "There is a kind of person who studies Ch'an like stuffing cakes in a crystal pitcher; it can't be turned over any more, it can't be cleaned out, and if you bump it, it immediately breaks. If you want to be lively and active, just study 'leather bag' Ch'an: even if you smash it down from the highest mountain, it still won't break, it won't burst." An Ancient said, "Even if you can grasp it before it is spoken, this is still remaining in the shell, wandering within limitation; even if you can thoroughly penetrate upon hearing a phrase, you still won't avoid crazy views on the way."

"How lamentable, laughable old T'ien P'ing; after all he says it was regrettable at the outset to go travelling." Hsueh Tou is saying that it's lamentable that he couldn't explain to others; it's laughable that he understood a bellyful of Ch'an but couldn't go on to make even the slightest use of it. "Wrong, wrong!" Some say that T'ien P'ing didn't understand, and thus was wrong; and some say his not speaking was wrong. But what connection is there? They hardly realize that these two "wrong"s are like stone struck sparks, like flashing lightning;

this is where those transcendent people tread, like using a sword to kill people, immediately grabbing people's throats, whereupon their root of life is severed. If you can travel on the sword's edge, then you will be free in all ways. If you can understand these two "wrong"s, then you can thereby see Hsi Yuan's pure wind suddenly melting (T'ien P'ing). When Hsueh Tou had finished quoting this story in the hall, he meant to say "wrong." I ask you, how does this wrong of Hsueh Tou compare to T'ien P'ing's wrong? Study for thirty more years.

TRANSLATORS' NOTES

a. According to the recommendation of Tenkei Denson, this pointer has been exchanged with that of the hundredth case, but either is suitable for both.

b. A man searching a battlefield for his father's remains finds a saddle ridge and mistakes it for his father's lower jaw.

Su Tsung's Ten-Body Controller

POINTER

When a dragon howls, mist arises; when a tiger roars, wind arises. In the fundamental design of appearing in the world, gold and jade[a] play together; in the strategic action of omnicompetence, arrowpoints meet each other.[b] The whole world is not concealed, far and near are equally revealed, past and present are clearly described.

But tell me, whose realm is this? To test, I cite this to see.

CASE

Emperor Su Tsung asked National Teacher Chung, "What is the Ten-Body Controller?"[1]

The National Teacher said, "Patron, walk on Vairocana's head."[2]

The emperor said, "I don't understand."[3]

The National Teacher said, "Don't acknowledge your own pure body of reality."[4]

NOTES

1. An adept ruler, the emperor of Great T'ang; he too should know this. On his head is the rolled lobe hat, on his feet are unworn shoes.
2. He takes his hand and walks together with him on the other side of Mount Sumeru. There is still this.
3. Why don't you understand his words? What a pity! The details are not imparted. The emperor should have immediately shouted then; what further need did he have to understand?
4. Although he makes complications, he still has a way to get himself out. Drunk and doddering, he saddens others to death.

COMMENTARY

When the Emperor Su Tsung was living in the Eastern Palace (as crown prince) he was already studying under National Teacher Chung. Later, when he succeeded to the throne, he honored him even more earnestly; when (Chung) came and went, (Su Tsung) greeted and saw him off, personally bearing the palanquin.

One day he posed a question to ask the National Teacher, "What is the Ten-Body Controller?" The Teacher said, "Patron, walk on Vairocana's head." The National Teacher's spine was usually as stiff as cast iron; but when he came into the presence of the emperor, it was like soft mud. Although he answered subtly, still he had a good point. He said, "If you want to understand, Patron, you must walk on Vairocana's head before you can understand." The emperor didn't get it; he said, "I don't understand." The National Teacher was subsequently extremely indulgent and entered into the weeds; he further commented on the preceding phrase by saying, "Do not mistakenly acknowledge your own pure body of reality." That refers to what is inherent in everyone, complete and perfect in each and every one. See how (Chung) lets go and gathers in, taking on adversaries from all sides.

Have you not heard it said that one who is good as a teacher sets up the teaching according to potential? He observes the wind to set the sail; if he just stayed in one corner, how could he interchange? Observe the Elder of Huang Po; he was well able to guide people; when he met Lin Chi, in three times he hit him sixty painful blows, and Lin Chi thereupon understood. But when he came to helping Prime Minister P'ei Hsiu, it was complicated in the extreme.[c] Was he not good as a teacher of people? National Teacher Chung skillfully used appropriate methods to teach Emperor Su Tsung; in all it was because he had the skill to take on adversaries from all sides. The "Ten-Body Controller" is the ten kinds of other-experienced body.[d] The three bodies of Reality *(dharmakaya)*, Enjoyment *(sambhogakaya)*, and Appearance *(nirmanakaya)*, are identical to the body of reality. Why? Because the enjoyment and appearance are not the real Buddha, and they are not what expounds the Dharma. When remaining in the body of reality, then as a single expanse of empty solidity, spiritual brightness quiescently shines.

When the Elder Fu of T'ai Yuan was expounding the *Nirvana* scripture in Kuang Hsiao Temple of Yang Chou, there was a wandering monk—actually it was the cook of Chia Shan—who was staying in the temple, snowed in; he took the opportunity to go listen to the lecture. When the lecture touched on the three bases of Buddha nature[e] and the three qualities of the body of reality,[f] and as Fu spoke profusely of the subtle principle of the body of reality, the cook suddenly broke out laughing. Fu then looked at him. When the lecture was over, he had someone summon the Ch'an man, and asked him, "My simple knowledge is narrow and inferior; I interpret the meanings according to the words. Just now, in the course of the lecture, I saw you break out in a laugh; I must have some shortcoming—please explain it to me."

The cook said, "If you did not ask, I dare not speak. Since you have asked, I cannot but explain. I was actually laughing because you don't know the body of reality." Fu said, "What is wrong with my explanation, such as it was?" The cook said, "Please explain it once more." Fu said, "The principle of the body of reality is like the great void: vertically, it goes through past, present, and future; horizontally it extends throughout the ten directions of the universe; it fills the eight extremities and embraces both positive and negative modes. According to conditions, it tends toward effect; there is nowhere it does not extend." The cook said, "I did not say your explanation is wrong; but you only know that which pertains to the extent of the body of reality; you do not actually know the body of reality." Fu said, "Granting that you are right, you should explain it for me." The cook said, "If you agree, then give up lecturing for ten days, and meditate correctly in a quiet room; collect your mind, gather your thoughts, give up various clingings to good and bad all at once, and investigate exhaustively on your own."

Fu did just as he had said, from the first to the fifth watch of the night; when he heard the sounding of the drum, he suddenly attained enlightenment and immediately went to knock on the Ch'an man's door. The cook said, "Who's there?" Fu said, "Me." The cook scolded him, saying "I would have you transmit and maintain the Great Teaching, explaining it in the

Buddha's stead; why are you laying in the street drunk on wine
in the middle of the night?" Fu said, "Hitherto in my lectures
on the scriptures I have been twisting the nostrils of the father
and mother who gave birth to me; from today on, I no longer
dare to be like this."

See that outstanding fellow! Did he merely go accept this
radiant spirituality and fall in front of asses but behind horses?
He had to have broken up his habitual active consciousness, so
that there is nothing that can be apprehended; yet he has still
only realized one half. An Ancient said, "If you do not give rise
to any thought of practice or study, within formless light you'll
always be free." Just discern that which is always silent and
still; do not acknowledge sound and form; just discern spiritual
knowledge, do not acknowledge false imagination. This is why
it was said, "Even if an iron wheel is turning on your head,
with concentration and wisdom complete and clear, they are
never lost."

Bodhidharma asked the Second Patriarch, "What did you cut
your arm off for, standing there in the snow?" The Patriarch
said, "My mind is not yet at ease; please ease my mind for me,
Master." Bodhidharma said, "Bring me your mind and I'll ease
it for you." The Patriarch said, "When I seek my mind, after all
I can't find it." Bodhidharma said, "I have eased your mind for
you." The Second Patriarch suddenly attained enlightenment.
But tell me, at just such a moment, where is the body of reality? Ch'ang Sha said,

> Students of the Way do not know reality
> Just because they acknowledge the conscious spirit
>   as before;
> It's the root of countless aeons of birth and death,
> Yet fools call it the original man.

People right now just acknowledge this radiant awareness, and
immediately stare and glare, playing with their spirits: but
what relevance does this have? As he said, "Do not acknowledge your own pure body of reality," but when it comes to your
own body of reality, you have still not even seen it in a dream;
how can you yet talk about not acknowledging it? In the doc-
trinal schools, they consider the pure body of reality to be the
ultimate law; why not let people acknowledge it? Haven't you
heard it said, "As long as you are acknowledging it, as before it

632   THE BLUE CLIFF RECORD

is after all still not so." Bah! It's best to immediately strike a
blow. Whoever can understand the meaning of this will for the
first time understand his saying, "Don't acknowledge your
own pure body of reality." Hsueh Tou dislikes his indulgent
kindness, but nevertheless there are thorns in the soft mud.

Have you not seen how Master Tung Shan had three roads
for teaching people? They were called the "Hidden Road," the
"Bird's Path," and "Extending the Hands." Beginners in the
study of the Way temporarily travelled the three roads. A monk
asked the Master, "You always teach students to travel the
Bird's Path: what is the Bird's Path like?" Tung Shan said,
"You don't meet anyone." The monk asked, "How can I travel
it?" Shan said, "There just should not be a single thread under
your feet as you go."ᵍ The monk said, "If I travel the Bird's
Path, is this not my Original Face?" Shan said, "Why are you
upside down?" The monk said, "How am I upside down?"
Shan said, "If you are not upside down, why do you take the
servant to be the master?" The monk said, "What is the Original Face?" Shan said, "It does not travel the Bird's Path."

You must see as far as this realm; only then will you have a
little realization. Even if you cleaned everything and made
yourself cut off your tracks and swallow your voice, still in the
school of the patchrobed monks this is still the view of novices
and children. You must still turn your heads around to the
troubles of the world and fully arouse your great function.

VERSE

"The Teacher of a Nation" is also a forced name;
    What is the necessity? A flower in the sky; the moon in
    the water. When the wind passes over, the treetops move.

Nan Yang alone may flaunt his good fame:
    After all he cuts off the essential bridge. Among a
    thousand or ten thousand, it's hard to find one or a half.

In Great T'ang he helped a real son of heaven—
    Pitiful. What is the use of teaching him? What is ac-
    complished by teaching a blind patchrobed monk?

Once he had him tread upon Vairocana's head.
    Why doesn't everybody go like this? They would find
    heaven and earth. How would you tread?

Then his iron hammer struck and shattered the golden bones;
   He's happy in everyday life. It's already thus before saying
   so.

Between heaven and earth, what more is there?
   Within the fast and boundless four oceans, there are few
   who know. The whole body bears the load. He is scatter-
   ing sand and dirt.

*The lands and seas of three thousand worlds by night are still
      and silent;*
   Set your eyes high. Hold fast to your territory; are you
   waiting to enter a ghost cave?

I do not know who enters the Blue Dragon's cave.
   Thirty blows of the staff; not one can be omitted. He's
   finished bringing it up, but do you understand? Bah!
   People, your nostrils have been pierced by Hsueh Tou. Do
   not mistakenly acknowledge your own pure body of reality.

COMMENTARY

"The Teacher of a Nation is also a forced name; / Nan Yang
alone may flaunt his good fame." This verse is just like a eu-
logy on a portrait. Haven't you heard it said that the ultimate
man has no name? To call him National Teacher is also a case
of having forcibly affixed a name. The Way of the National
Teacher is incomparable. He was skillfully able to teach others
in this way.

   Nan Yang alone may be accepted as a Master: "In Great
T'ang he helped a true son of heaven, and once had him tread
upon Vairocana's head." If you have the eye and brain of a
patchrobed monk who possesses the eye, you must walk upon
Vairocana's head, and only then will you see this Ten-Body
Controller. A Buddha is called the "Controller"; this is one of
his ten epithets.[h] One body transforms into ten bodies, ten
bodies transform into a hundred bodies, and so on, to a
thousand hundred hundred million bodies; in their totality
they are just one body. This one verse is easy to explain; the
latter versifies that saying, "Do not acknowledge your pure

body of reality," and versifies in sucha way that water poured on cannot wet it; it is difficult to explain.

"His iron hammer strikes, smashing the golden bones." This versifies "Do not acknowledge your own pure body of reality." Hsueh Tou praises (Chung) greatly; the golden bones have been smashed by one blow of his mallet. "Between heaven and earth, what more is there?" It is just necessary to be clean and naked, bare and untrammelled, so there is no longer anything to be apprehended; then this is the scenery of the basic ground. It is just like the lands and seas of three thousand worlds still and silent in the night. In a universe of three thousand great world systems, in the midst of the Sea of Fragrant Waters, there are infinite lands; in each land there is an ocean. Just when the night is deep and still, and heaven and earth are at once clear and calm, tell me, what is this? Just don't make an understanding of closing your eyes. If you understand in this way, then you'll fall into the poisonous sea.

"I don't know who enters the Blue Dragon's cave." Stretching out the legs, folding the legs; tell me, who is this? Everybody's nostrils have been pierced by Hsueh Tou all at once.

TRANSLATORS' NOTES

a. "Gold" means an instrument made of metal; "jade," an instrument of stone: ancient Chinese music began with "gold" and ended with "jade"—hence "gold and jade" refers to "consummation." Also they are used to indicate excellence, so we translate literally.

b. This refers to two master archers shooting at each other; their skill is equal, so their arrows meet each other midway and stop. This story is originally from the *Lieh-tzu,* a Taoist classic; there is also the famous passage in Shih T'ou's *Ts'an T'ung Ch'i* which says, "Phenomena's existence is like box and cover joining; principles' correspondence is like arrowpoints meeting."

c. This refers to the *Ch'uan Hsin Fa Yao,* "Essentials of the Method of Transmission of Mind," addresses of Huang Po recorded by P'ei Hsiu. Being for a layman, they are quite different from Huang Po's dealings with monks.

d. A Buddha is said to have two kinds of real body *(dharmakaya)*; that experienced by himself, and that experienced by others. The former is his own enlightenment, and the latter is his teaching of others, or how others experience the Buddha in their perceptions of his qualities and teachings. According to the *Hua Yen,* or Flower Garland scripture, there are the Buddha of nonattachment, the Buddha of vows, the Buddha of results of action, the Buddha of abiding maintenance, the Buddha of extinction *(nirvana),* the Buddha of the cosmos (the *dharmadhatu,* or ultimate realm), the Buddha of mind, the Buddha of concentration, the Buddha of nature, and the magical Buddha. Vairocana, the Great Illuminator, also called the Great Sun Buddha in Chinese, is the primordial Buddha, representing the body of reality, the basis and totality of all these.

e. The three bases of Buddha nature are the true basis, the basis of understanding, and the basis of conditions. The true basis is the real nature which underlies Buddhahood, the Buddha nature inherent in everyone; the basis of understanding is wisdom, which realizes this real nature; the basis of conditions is the practices which unfold wisdom and allow one to realize one's Buddha nature.

f. The three qualities of the body of reality correspond to the three bases of Buddha nature; the quality of the pure body of reality, which corresponds to the true basis, the quality of wisdom, which corresponds to the basis of understanding, and the quality of liberation, which corresponds to the basis of conditions, cultivation of liberating practices.

g. Even the most ancient texts give an alternative reading which is homonymous; "Nothing private under your feet." For an explanation of the three roads of Tung Shan, see the appropriate appendix.

h. The ten epithets of a Buddha are, Realized One (Tathagata), Worthy (Arhat), True and Universal Knower, Perfect in Knowledge and Conduct, Blissful One, Understander of the World, Unexcelled Knight, Controller of Humanity, Teacher of Humans and Gods, Enlightened One (Buddha), World Honored One. The translations given here are based on Chinese; the Sanskrit equivalents given in parentheses are those which are frequently used in English books.

Pa Ling's Blown Hair Sword

POINTER

All summer I've been verbosely making up complications, and almost entangled and tripped up all the monks in the land. But when the Diamond Sword cuts directly, I first realize my hundred-fold incompetence. But tell me, what is the Diamond Sword like? Open your eyes and I'll reveal the swordpoint for you to see.

CASE

A monk asked Pa Ling, "What is the Blown Hair Sword?"[1a]
Pa Ling said, "Each branch of coral supports the moon."[2]

NOTES

1. Cut! Dangerous!
2. The light engulfs myriad forms, the entire land.

COMMENTARY

Pa Ling does not move his shield and spear, (but) in the land, how many people's tongues fall to the ground! Yun Men taught people just like this; (Pa Ling) was a true son of Yun Men. And each of (Yun Men's successors) had his strategy of action; that is why (Hsueh Tou) said, "I always admire Shao Yang's newly established devices; all his life he pulled out nails and drew out pegs for people."

This story is just like this; within one phrase there are three phrases naturally inherent—the phrase enclosing heaven and earth, the phrase cutting off all streams, and the phrase following the waves. His reply was undeniably outstanding. Yuan "the jurist" of Fu Shan said, "For a man who has not yet passed through, studying the meaning is not as good as studying the phrase." At Yun Men's place there were three venerable adepts who replied about the "Blown Hair Sword"; two of them said, "Complete." Only Pa Ling was able to give an answer beyond the word "complete"—this is attaining the phrase.

But tell me, are "complete" and "each branch of coral supports the moon" the same or different? Before, (Hsueh Tou) said, "The three phrases should be distinguished; one arrow flies through space." If you want to understand this story, you must cut off the defilement of feelings and conscious conceptions, and be completely purified; then you will see his saying, "Each branch of coral supports the moon." If you make up any further rationalization, all the more you'll find you're unable to grasp it.

These words are from Ch'an Yueh's poem of remembering a friend:

> Thick as the iron on the Iron Closure Mountains,
> Thin as the dapples on the body of immortal Shuang Cheng.
> Pheonixes and fowl from the looms of Shu always make him stumble.
> Each branch of coral supports the moon;
> Stored away in the house of Wang K'ai, it is hard to dig out.
> Yen Hui, that hungry fellow, laments the sky's snow;
> The ancient cypress brush is so straight, even snow can't break it.
> The snow-clad stone girl's curling peach belt—
> Wearing it, he enters the dragon palace, his steps slow.
> The embroidered screen, the silver ladle; how do they differ?
> The jet black dragon has lost the jewel; do you know it or not?

Pa Ling took one phrase from among these lines to reply to the "Blown Hair Sword"; he is quick. One blows a hair against the edge of a sword to test it; when the hair splits of itself, then it is a sharp sword, and it is called a blown hair sword. Pa Ling just goes to the point of his question and immediately answers this monk's words. (The monk's) head fell without him even realizing it.

VERSE

When it is necessary to even the uneven,
    Tiny as an ant. A powerful man should be like this.

Even the great adept seems inept.
    He does not stir sound or form. He hides his body but reveals his shadow.

Sometimes on the finger, sometimes in the palm;
    Look! After all this is not it.

Leaning against the sky, it shines on the snow—
    Cut! If you stare at it, you'll go blind.

Even a great smith cannot hone it;
    What do you still want to forget it for? Even Kan Chiang (the legendary smith) couldn't find it.

Even a master craftsman wouldn't finish polishing it.
    No one could do it. Even if Kan Chiang came forth, he too would fall back.

It is exceptional, unique:
    Bah! What is so special about it? (Yet) there is something praiseworthy about it.

Each branch of coral supports the moon.
    In the third watch the moon descends, its image shining in the cold pond. Tell me, where does it go? Drunk and doddering, he saddens others to death.

COMMENTARY

"When it is necessary to even the uneven, the great adept seems inept." In the past there were wandering warriors; on their way when they saw inequity where the strong oppressed the weak, then they would let fly with their swords to take the heads of the strong. Thus, masters of our school hide a jewel sword in their eyebrows, and hang a golden mallet in their sleeves, whereby to settle matters of unrest. "The great adept seems inept"—Pa Ling's answer was intended to even what was uneven; because his words were exceeding skillful, instead they turn out to seem inept. What is the reason? Because he does not come attack directly: instead he goes off into a corner and with one stroke secretly beheads the man, yet the man is not aware of it.

"Sometimes on the finger, sometimes in the palm; / Leaning against the sky, it shines on the snow." If you can understand, then it is like the cold and severe spiritual grandeur of a long sword leaning against the sky. An Ancient said, "The mind moon solitary and full, its light engulfs myriad forms. The light is not shining on objects, and the objects are not existing, either. Light and objects both forgotten, then what is this?" This jewel sword is sometimes manifest on the fingertip; suddenly it appears in the palm. In the old days when Librarian Ch'ing had reached this point in his explanation, he raised his hand and said, "Do you see?" Still, it's not necessarily in the hand or the finger: Hsueh Tou just takes a shortcut to let you see the Ancient's meaning. But say, every place cannot but be the Blown Hair Sword; that is why it is said, "When the waves are high at the triple gate, the fish turn to dragons; yet foolish people still drag the evening pond water."

Hsueh Tou says this sword can lean against the sky and shine upon the snow. Usually it is said that the light of the long sword leaning against the sky can shine on the snow: this little bit of function is such that even a great smith cannot hone it, even a master craftsman could never finish polishing it. The master craftsman is such as Nan Chiang (the legendary expert smith): the old tale is self-evident.[b]

When Hsueh Tou has finished the verse, in the end he reveals (the sword), saying, "Exceptional, unique!" It is undeniably exceptional, and has special excellence; it is not like an ordinary sword. But tell me, how is it special? "Each branch of coral supports the moon." This can be said to be prior to light and after annihilation, occupying the heartland alone, without any peer.

Ultimately, how is it? People, your heads are fallen. I have one more little verse:

Filling a boat with ten thousand bushels, I let you
haul it away;
Instead, for one grain of rice, the pot has entrapped
the snake.
Having brought up one hundred old public cases,
How much sand have I thrown in people's eyes to-
day?

TRANSLATORS' NOTES

a. As usual, the sword symbolizes wisdom, cutting off confusion and attachment; uncontrived and equanimous, it sees the moon of truth everywhere in everything.
b. There is a story inserted in the text about Kan Chiang, the legendary smith, and how he made the famous sword No Yeh. All commentaries reject it as a later addition, and it serves no purpose except to identify the name of Kan Chiang.

Biographical Supplement

The order of the biographies is as follows:

CH'ANG KUAN of Wu Feng (n.d.)
CASE 70,71

(Wu Feng was one of Pai Chang's successors; the following is from the *Ching Te Ch'uan Teng Lu* 9:)

There was a monk who asked, "What is the scenery (or: perspective) of Wu Feng?" The master said, "Dangerous." The monk asked, "What is the man within the scene?" The master said, "A block."

The master said to a monk who was taking leave of him, "Where are you going, Reverend?" The monk said, "I'm going to Mt. T'ai." The master raised one finger and said, "If you see Manjusri, return here and I'll meet with you." (Traditionally, Mt. T'ien T'ai was an abode of Manjusri.) The monk had no reply.

The master asked a monk, "Have you seen the ox?" The monk said he had seen it. The master said, "Did you see the left horn or the right horn?" The monk had no reply. The master answered himself on his behalf, "I saw that there was no left or right."

641

Another monk was taking leave of the master, who said to him, "When you go all over, don't slander me (by saying that) I am here." The monk said, "I won't say you're here." The master said, "Where would you say I am?" The monk held up one finger. The master said, "You have already slandered me."

T'AN SHENG of Yun Yen (781–841)
CASE 72, 89

(The following is from the *Ching Te Ch'uan Teng Lu* 14:)

He was from Chien Ch'ang in Chung Ling; his surname was Wang. At an early age he left home. At first he studied under Ch'an Master Hai of Pai Chang, but he did not awaken to his mystic meaning. After he had served Pai Chang for around twenty years, Pai Chang died so Yun Yen visited Yao Shan and reached understanding there at his words. . . . Later the master dwelt at Yun Yen Shan ("Cloud Cliff Mountain") in T'an Chou (in Hunan).

One day Yun Yen told the assembly, "There's a son of someone's family—when questioned, there is nothing he cannot explain." Tung Shan asked, "How many scriptures were there in his house?" The master said, "Not even a single word." "Then how did he get so much knowledge?" The master said, "Day and night he never slept." "Could I still ask him about something?" The master said, "If he could say, he wouldn't say."

Once when Yun Yen was sweeping the floor, Kuei Shan said to him, "Too busy!" The master said, "You should know that there's one who isn't busy." Kuei Shan said, "If so, then there's a second moon." The master held up his broom and said "Which moon is this?" Kuei Shan lowered his head and left. When Hsuan Sha heard of this he said, "Precisely the second moon."

Once when Yun Yen was making shoes, Tung Shan asked, "If I come to you, Master, and ask for eyes, I wonder, will I get them or not?" Yun Yen said, "Who did you give yours to?" Tung Shan said, "I haven't got any." The master said, "If you had, where would you put them?" Tung Shan was speechless. The master said, "Is the one asking for eyes an eye or not?" Tung Shan said, "He's not an eye." The master scoffed at him.

In 841 in the tenth month the master showed illness. On the twenty-sixth, after he had washed, he called the Superintendent Monk and ordered him to prepare a feast. On the twenty-seventh when evening came the master returned to quiescence.

CHIH TSANG of Hsi T'ang (734–814)
CASE 73

(The following is taken from the *Ching Te Ch'uan Teng Lu* 7:)
The master was originally from Ch'ien Hua; his surname was Liao. From age eight he followed a teacher; at twenty-five he was fully ordained. Someone who met him noticed his special appearance and said to him, "Your mettle is not commonplace: you ought to be the Dharma King's helper." So the master went to Buddha's Footprint Range to visit Ma Tsu and pay his respects. There he entered Ma Tsu's room along with Ch'an Master Hai of Pai Chang: both received Ma Tsu's seal.

One day Ma Tsu sent the master to Ch'ang An to present a book to National Teacher Chung. The National Teacher asked, "What Dharma does your master expound?" Hsi T'ang crossed from east to west and stood there. The National Teacher said, "What else is there besides just this?" The master recrossed to the east and stood there. The National Teacher said, "This is Ma Tsu's; what about you, good man?" The master said, "There's already been a showing for you, Teacher."

Hsi T'ang returned to his native district: he had received Ma Tsu's patched robe.... One day Ma Tsu asked him, "Why don't you read sutras?" The master said, "Could sutras be any different (from this)?" Ma Tsu said, "Though this is so, later on you'll still have to help people." The master said, "I am sick and want to heal myself: how could I dare to speak for others?" Ma Tsu said, "In your last years you will inevitably (cause the Dharma to) flourish in the world." After Ma Tsu had died, the congregation in 791 asked the master to open the hall (and teach).

Hsi T'ang died in 814 at the age of 80: he had been a monk for fifty-five years. (Two T'ang emperors,) Hsien Tsung and Mu Tsung bestowed posthumous titles on him.

TING CHOU SHIH TSANG (714–800)

(The record says he was entombed in a memorial tower in 800, but it is not clear just when he died.)

CASE 75

(No biography of this master is recorded in the sectarian Ch'an histories; the information given here is taken from the *Sung Kao Seng Chuan*, 10.)

When young, the master studied Confucianism; later he entered the Buddhist order, and went to study under the renowned P'u Chi (who was known as the Seventh Patriarch in the northern Ch'an tradition; his master had been Shen Hsiu, one of the Fifth Patriarch Hung Jen's ten great disciples). There he was enlightened in Ch'an; later he came to Great Elephant Peak in the mountains of central China, where he sat alone peacefully in deep nirvanic stillness for several years. Students came seeking him out and gathered around him; eventually Li T'ao Ying, military commander of Hui Cou and member of the imperial clan, ordered him to come to the city; but Shih Tsang refused, saying that his rustic nature was impossible to bridle, and he couldn't be bothered with rules of etiquette. Li then climbed the mountain himself to talk to the Master; afterwards, he petitioned the throne to grant a title to Shih Tsang's abode, but Shih Tsang had already taken leave of his disciples, and passed on the next day.

The master Wu Chiu ('Crow's Nest'), who figures in case 75, is obscure, but it seems he was a successor of Ma Tsu (709–788).

T'IEN JAN of Tan Hsia (738–824)

CASE 76

(A successor to Shih T'ou, Tan Hsia was the "father" of Ts'ui Wei and thus the "grandfather" of T'ou Tzu. The following is related in the *Ching Te Ch'uan Ten Lu* 14:)

It is not known what locality the master was from. At first he studied Confucianism, intending to go to Ch'ang An to take part in the imperial examinations. (What happened to him on the road that made him turn to Buddhism, as well as the circumstances of his meetings with Ma Tsu and Shih T'ou, is told by Yuan Wu in Case 76.) After he returned to Ma Tsu's after having his head shaved by Shih T'ou, Ma Tsu asked, "Where did you come here from?" Tan Hsia said, "Shih T'ou." Ma Tsu said, "Shih T'ou's road is slippery: did he trip you up?" The master said, "If he had, I wouldn't have come."

Next the master went travelling to look over the various localities (where Ch'an flourished). For three years he lived on Mt. T'ien T'ai's Flower Top Peak. He went to Hang Chou's Ching Shan and payed his respects to Ch'an Master Kuo I. In the middle of the Yuan Ho years (806–821) he went to the Dragon Gate (Mountain's) Fragrant Mountain near Loyang, where he and Master Fu Niu were faithful friends.... He also visited National Teacher Chung....

(One day during the year) 809 the master stretched out on T'ien Chin Bridge. When the governor, Lord Cheng, appeared, the master reviled him and didn't get up. One of the governor's attendants asked him his reason for doing this. The master took his time about answering and said, "(Because I am) an unconcerned monk." The governor considered him extraordinary and offered him clothes and daily provisions of food. In the spring of his fifteenth year (in Loyang) the master announced to his disciples, "I've been thinking of a place with forests and streams in which to die." Soon his disciples had a geomancer (pick a site for) a hermitage to be built on Tan Hsia Mountain in Nan Yang. Within three years time (after the master had taken up residence there) students of the mystery had gathered, forming a congregation of three hundred, so they built a monastery.

WEI YEN of Yao Shan (750–834)
CASE 81

(Yeo Shan was a successor to Shih T'ou and the ancestor of the Ts'ao-Tung School. The following comes from the *Te Ching Ch'uan Teng Lu* 14:)

Ch'an Master Wei Yen of Yao Shan in Li Chou (in Hunan) was a man from Chiang Chou (in Shansi); his surname was

Han. He left home at age seventeen and was ordained in 774 on Heng Yueh by the Vinaya Master Hsi Ts'ao.

As soon as he visited Shih T'ou, the master intimately comprehended his esoteric message. One day as the master was sitting, Shih T'ou saw him and asked, "What are you doing here?" The master said, "I'm not doing anything at all." Shih T'ou said, "If so then you're sitting idly." The master said, "If I were sitting idly, that would be doing something." Shih T'ou said, "You speak of not doing: not doing what?" The master said, "Even the thousand sages do not know." Shih T'ou praised him with a verse:

> Since we've lived together I haven't known your
> name.
> Doing as you please, acting this way, bringing me
> along—
> Even the sages of high antiquity don't know:
> How could the hurried common type be able to understand.

Shih T'ou once said, "Speech and action have nothing to do with it." The master said, "Not speaking and non-action don't have anything to do with it either." Shih T'ou said, "Here, not even a needle can enter." The master said, "Here, it's like growing flowers on stone." Shih T'ou approved of him. Later the master dwelt on Yao Shan in Li Chou: an oceanlike congregation gathered.

A monk asked, "How can one not be confused by all phenomena?" The master said, "If you go along with them, how can they obstruct you?" The monk said, "I don't understand." The master said, "What phenomena are confusing you?"

A monk asked, "What is *nirvana?*" The master said, "What did you call it before you opened your mouth?"

A monk asked, "I have not yet understood my own thing: please, Teacher, point it out to me." After a silence the master said, "It wouldn't be hard for me to say something for you right now: it would only be proper if you immediately saw at my words—then you'd have gotten somewhere. But if you kept on entering into calculating thought, it would become my fault. It's not as good as both of us shutting up to avoid entangling each other."

As Yao Shan was about to die he cried out, "The Dharma Hall is collapsing! The Dharma Hall is collapsing! Everybody prop it up!" Then he raised his hand and said, "You disciples don't understand my meaning," and died.

CH'I AN of Yen Kuan (District's) Chen Kuo Hai Ch'ang Temple

(The following is taken from the *Ching Te Ch'uan Teng Lu* 7:)

Yen Kuan was originally from Hai Men District (in Chekiang); his surname was Li. When he was born a spiritual light filled the room. Also, there was a strange monk who told him, "Will you not be the one who will establish the supreme banner and make the Buddha-sun shine back?" So he had his head shaved and was ordained by Ch'an Master Yun Tsung of his native district. Later he heard that Ma Tsu was teaching on Kung Kung Mountain, so he took his staff and went to visit him there. Yen Kuan had an extraordinary appearance: as soon as Ma Tsu saw him he considered him a profound vessel, so he ordered him to come into his room and intimately instructed him in the Correct Dharma.

A monk asked Yen Kuan, "What is one's own Vairocana Buddha?" The master said, "Bring me that brass pitcher." The monk then brought the pitcher over. The master said, "Take it back and put it where it was." Having returned the pitcher to its place, this monk came back to ask again about his previous question. Yen Kuan said, "The ancient Buddha is indeed long gone!"

A lecturing monk came calling. The master asked him, "What is your work?" The lecturer said, "I lecture on the Hua Yen sutra." The master said, "How many kinds of dharma worlds are there in the sutra?" The lecturer answered, "To explain fully, there are many many, without end; to explain briefly, there are four kinds." The master held up his whisk and said, "Which kind of dharma world is this?" The lecturer sank into thought as he slowly pondered his reply. The master said, "To know by pondering, to understand by thinking it over—

this is the way ghosts make their living. Sure enough, the lone lamp beneath the sun loses its glow."

A monk asked Ta Mei, "What is the meaning of the coming from the West?" Ta Mei said, "The coming from the West has no meaning." When Yen Kuan heard of this he said, "One coffin, two corpses."

Later, without illness, Yen Kuan sat peacefully and died.

CHÜ HUI of Ta Kuang (836–903)
CASE 93

(The following is taken from the account in the *Ching Te Ch'uan Teng Lu* 16:)

The master was a man from the capital district (Ch'ang An); his surname was Wang.

When he first visited the room of Shih Shuang (his master) he passed two years staying close by, asking for instruction. He was ordered to take charge of the North Stupa. With clothes of hemp and shoes of straw, he was on the verge of forgetting his body and consciousness. One day Shih Shuang, intending to test what Ta Kuang had attained, questioned him saying, "Every year the country sends its chosen candidates to compete in the examinations: do they get posts at court or not?" The master said, "There are people who do not seek advancement." Shih Shuang said, "Why?" The master said, "Because they do not act for the sake of fame." While he was ill, Shih Shuang again questioned the master, "Is there any other time besides Today?" The master said, "I don't even say Today is right." Shih Shuang approved of him very much. . . . The master stayed in the vicinity (of Shih Shuang) for over twenty years.

The benefactor of Buddhism, Lord Hu of Liu Yang (in Hunan), invited the master to reside on Mt. Ta Kuang, in order to propagate the teachings of the sect.

There was a monk who asked, "As for Bodhidharma, was he a Patriarch or not?" Ta Kuang said, "He wasn't a Patriarch." The monk said, "Since he wasn't a Patriarch, what did he come for?" The master said, "Because you wouldn't comprehend a Patriarch." The monk asked, "What's it like after comprehending?" The master said, "You finally know he wasn't a Patriarch."

The master was asked, "What was it like during the primordial chaos, before differentiation?" The master said, "Who can relate the Teachings of the Age?" The master also said, "The Teachings of the Age were just to straighten out the people of the age. Even if you can cut all the way through them, this is just becoming a person who has finished his task. You shouldn't then take this as the business of patchrobed ones." Thus it is said, "In forty-nine years Buddha couldn't explain it fully; in forty-nine years he couldn't wrap it all up." Whenever Ta Kuang taught students it was generally like this.

SSU MING of Hsi Yuan in Ju Chou (in Honan) (n.d.)
CASE 98

(Ssu Ming succeeded to Master Chao of Pao Chou, a disciple of Lin Chi; he had one successor. The following dialogues are taken from *Ching Te Ch'uan Teng Lu* 12:)

Someone asked, "What is a monastery?"

The master said, "A forest of thorns."

He asked, "What is the man in the monastery?"

The master said, "A boar; a badger."

Someone asked, "What is the one shout of Lin Chi?"

The master said, "A thirty-thousand-pound catapult is not shot at a rat."

He said, "Where is the master's compassion?"

The master hit him.

Tsung I of T'ien P'ing Mountain, also in Honan, who also appears in case 98, has no separate record in any of the classical histories; he was a successor of Ch'ing Ch'i Hung Chin, a disciple of Lo Han Kuei Ch'en and former travelling companion of Fa Yen Wen I.

Select Glossary of Names and Terms

alayavijnana—The so-called storehouse or repository consciousness, wherein accumulate influences of deed and habit, producing impressions which are customarily mistaken for qualities of the objective world; when all egoism and self-affirming habits of attachment are eliminated, this all embracing consciousness is 'transformed' into the so-called great perfect mirror knowledge.

Avalokitesvara—The bodhisattva representing compassion and all-sided skill in liberative technique, traditionally said to be the guardian of the compassion and love of Amitabha, Buddha of Infinite Light and Life. Known also as the Sound Seer from the image of the lord who watches the sounds of the world to rescue beings in distress; it is said in the Surangama scripture that Avalokitesvara attained enlightenment through audition by turning back to look into the source of hearing; this meditative exercise is well known and often applied in Ch'an practice.

Bodhidharma—The First Patriarch of Ch'an in China, said to have originally been of a noble Brahmin family from south India, later became the successor of Prajnatara, Twenty-seventh Patriarch of Buddhism, and spent fifty years in China after having already taught in India for sixty odd years.

bodhisattva—An enlightened being or a warrior for enlightenment, one who forgoes the repose of extinction to struggle for the enlightenment of all conscious beings, voluntarily accepting the passions and confusions of the mundane life in order to communicate with the beings involved there so as to be able to fulfill his commitment to liberate them.

Buddha—A completely enlightened one, also called one who has come to realize thusness, World Honored One, king of Dharma, teacher of humans and gods, lord.

Buddha Dharma—The teaching of the enlightened ones, the way to enlightenment; also used to refer to truth or reality.

consciousnesses—Refers to the fields and functions of consciousnesses associated with senses, intellection, judgment, and formation of habit, etc. Emotional consciousness is states of mind, emotion, and intellection, which are primarily influenced by emotions ('like' 'dislike' etc., which inevitably return to the attempt to preserve the idea or feeling of self) and thus screened by such involvements from clear perception of reality or truth.

demon—Representation of deluding or confusing forces, objects of attachment or aversion, or malevolent forces robbing people of clarity, will, and the life of wisdom.

diamond king—The awakened mind; diamond is a symbol of penetrating wisdom, indestructible as a diamond.

dragon—Someone who is enlightened or has reached an advanced spiritual degree; though 'dragons' live physically in the 'animal' world, their profound state of meditation allows them to transcend this condition and enjoy the bliss of heavenly states or complete calm. Great Ch'an adepts and students are often referred to as 'dragons and elephants'—one who looks adept at first but turns out otherwise is said to have a 'dragon's head but a snake's tail.'

Gaptooth—'He with gapped rotting teeth' is Bodhidharma (qv), also known as the Blue-Eyed Barbarian or the Red-Bearded Barbarian, the Pierced-Ear Traveller, the First Patriarch, the Ancestral Teacher; he is also referred to by place names such as Shao Lin, Few Houses (name of mountain where Shao Lin temple was), and Bear's Ear Mountain (where he is entombed).

Gautama—A Buddha, inspirator of Buddhism's historical forms and perhaps the greatest of known teachers of the way of enlightenment; also called Yellow Face and Old Shakyamuni.

jewel sword—Symbol of adamantine wisdom, transcendental knowing, which is able to cut through all confusion and delusion.

intimacy—Intimate communion with reality, personal experience of the Way.

It—The absolute (used both so as to contain the relative absolute and the absolute relative); reality, or what is. Often *It* is not specified in Chinese but needed in English to fit the sense. *This* (one, side) and *That* (one, side) are sometimes used to refer specifically to the imminent and transcendent aspects of *It*. *He* is also used similarly, like the Arabic *Hu*, a name for reality; in Ch'an usage, this can be read as personal ('there is nothing that is not the self of a saint') or impersonal ('a saint has no self').

kashaya—An upper vestment worn by monks when meditating or performing symbolic services.

Maitreya—The Loving One, the future Buddha, said to be presently living in the heaven of satisfaction, awaiting the time when he will be born on earth for the welfare of all beings. Mahasattva Fu (cf. case 67) and Pu Tai (Hotei) were both considered to be manifestations of Maitreya.

mahasattva—An enlightened bodhisattva, a great hero or great knight (the literal meaning of mahasattva) who is fully qualified for complete buddhahood, but travels endlessly in the rounds of life to liberate beings rather than abiding as the pole of a field of enlightenment. All the transhistorical bodhisattvas mentioned in the Blue Cliff Record are mahasattvas.

Mahasthamaprapta—The bodhisattva representing empowerment, depicted as the guardian of the knowledge of Amitabha Buddha.

Manjusri—The bodhisattva representing wisdom and knowledge, depicted as riding on a golden lion (symbol of the body of reality) and being the teacher of the seven Buddhas of antiquity. Manjusri's image is the conventional main icon of Ch'an meditation halls.

nirvana—Extinction of suffering, known as Peace, Liberation, Bliss, the Other Shore, the Refuge, the Uncompounded, etc. In early Buddhism *nirvana* was known as the correct, or absolute state, and is the essence of sainthood.

outsider—This is used by Buddhists to refer to non-Buddhists, but in Ch'an lingo anyone who seeks or grasps anything is called an outsider, estranged from inherent enlightened nature.

Patriarch—Ancestor; refers to living examples of enlightenment; it can refer to the leaders or founders of branches of Buddhism, and in Ch'an is also used as a term of respect for adepts of earlier generations as well as the founders of the streams.

patchrobe—An example and symbol of poverty, the clothes of Buddhist ascetics were made of patched rags. This expression is also used in Sufism, with the same basic sense.

pillar and lamp—Being present in the teaching halls, the pillar and lamp are often mentioned as examples and thus representative of the objective world.

reed shade—A bundle of reeds used to shade sun off water so as to be able to see beyond the surface into the depths—a simile for tactics of a Teaching Master to draw out or see into a student.

samadhi—One-pointed focus of mind; concentration or absorption; sometimes extended in Ch'an usage to refer to any state of mind, any activity, even phenomena.

Samantabhadra—Bodhisattva representing goodness and wisdom in all actions, the ultimate principle of union of knowledge and myriad deeds for the enlightenment of all beings; Samantabhadra is depicted as riding on an elephant. The vow of Samantabhadra closes the *Gandhavyuha*, a major scripture contained in the grand *Avatamsaka* (Hua Yen) scripture; it bespeaks the ultimate aspirations of those who conceive the will for universal enlightenment.

South—A code word for Ch'an study ('going South') or enlightened knowledge itself; the journey of Sudhana for enlightenment (which is the story of the *Gandhavyuha*) was to the South and Ch'an flourished most in southern China during its golden age in the T'ang dynasty—hence the association came to be a fixed term.

Tathagata—An epithet of Buddhas, meaning one who has come to realize thusness.

triple world—Three worlds; refers to the realms of desire, form, and formlessness or immateriality.

turning word—Word or expression occasioning or representing the transformation from delusion to enlightenment, especially a term or phrase which contains both ordinary and spiritual or transcendental meanings, both provisional and real, or both negative and positive modes.

triple vehicle—Three vehicles; refers to the careers of discipleship (following the Dharma to realize personal emptiness and sainthood), self-enlightenment (solitary liberation through understanding of the process of conditioning), and bodhisattvahood (realization of both personal and phenomenal emptiness and the conception of great compassion and commitment to the enlightenment of all beings). These three vehicles lead into the so-called unique vehicle, which is the way of complete Buddhahood.

Ts'ao Ch'i—A river and river valley in south China, where the famous Sixth Patriarch of Ch'an taught; hence it comes to be a codeword not only for that Patriarch, Hui Neng, but for all the streams of Ch'an (and hence Ch'an itself, after the ninth century) which were descended from Hui Neng's enlightened disciples.

whisk—Used for nonviolent insect dispersal, its use was a prerogative of abbots, so it came to be another symbol (and in fact was physically handed down as such) of the succession of a Ch'an lineage; it is commonly used, however, like the pillar and the lamp, as a representative symbol of This, objective reality.

Vairocana—The great Sun Buddha, the Illuminator, the so-called Adibuddha or primordial awakening, symbolizing the body of reality. As a meditation *(dhyani)* Buddha in esoteric Buddhism, Vairocana is associated with mind and may be said to represent the basic awakened intelligence or the fundamental luminous quality of awareness. The cosmos itself also may be said to be an attribute of Vairocana.

Guide to Chinese Pronunciation

According to the transcription method used in The Blue Cliff Record, *based on the modified Wade-Giles system*

Chinese	English approximation
a	father
ai	eye
ao	how
ch	j
ch'	ch
e	but (n.b. er(h) sounds like *are*, ei sounds like h*ay*)
f	f
h	h
i	p*i*n (ih sounds like h*er*)
hs	*s*ure
k	g
k'	k
l	l
m	m
n	n
o	b*u*t (only when whole syllable consists of o; otherwise, o sounds like th*aw*); ou sounds like thr*o*w
p	b
p'	p
r	no equivalent; resembles mix of French j and English r
s	s
sh	sh (palatalized hs)
sz	s (only in szu, which resembles *ce*rtain)

t	d
t'	t
ts	dz
ts'	ts
tz	dz (these two only before u; see sz)
tz'	ts
u	put (ui=*way*, ua=*wa*, uo=*waw*, ueh=*ywe*)
w	w
y	y

This does not exhaust the intricacies of Chinese phonetics but is intended to help the reader with a reasonably comfortable and accurate way of reading Chinese names.

Bibliography

The following early modern commentaries on the *Blue Cliff Record* by Japanese Zen Masters were also consulted in addition to the commentaries cited in the bibliography appended to volume 1;

Ashahina Sōgen, *Hekiganroku kōwa.* Tokyo, Kawade shobō, 1956.
Iida Tōin, *Hekiganshū teishōroku.* Tokyo Morikawa shoten, 1932.
Imazu Kōgaku *Heikiganshū Kōgi.* Tokyo, Mugazanbō, 1913.
Ōuchi Seiran, *Hekiganroku kōwa.* Tokyo, Kōmeisha, 1906.
Shaku Sōen, *Hekiganroku kōwa.* Tokyo, Kōyūkan, 1915–16.